A Season of Beholding
The Journey from Epiphany to Lent

Jim Branch

Truth sees God, and wisdom beholds God, and from these two comes the third, and that is a marvelous delight in God, which is love.

~Julian of Norwich

Introduction

The sixth of January marks the Feast of the Epiphany. It is the time in the church calendar when we, like the Magi, follow the star in order to *behold* the Christ. The word *epiphany* means a*n appearance or manifestation*, which makes it a time when we celebrate *seeing* Him — however, wherever, and whenever he may choose to appear.

"We must be very loving and very alert if we want to recognize Him in his earthly disguise," writes Evelyn Underhill. "Again and again He comes and the revelation is not a bit what we expect." Which means that if we really do want to see Jesus, then *beholding* him must become one of the chief occupations of our hearts and souls. Unfortunately, that's not as easy as it sounds; it takes practice.

"What is required," counsels Theophan the Recluse, "is a constant aliveness to God — an aliveness present when you talk, read, watch, or examine something." A vital attentiveness is necessary. An attentiveness and aliveness to God's movement and God's presence is essential. It is a state of being that's cultivated by prayer and nurtured by love; we must become people who have been seized by the power of his great affection. We must become people who constantly have an eye out for the living God. And once our hearts have been captured by his unfailing love, our eyes will follow. They will begin to see him everywhere.

So let us keep our eyes peeled and our hearts attentive. Let us sit in silence and read our scriptures and say our prayers. Let us stop and listen and reflect and journal, for these things make time and space within us to *behold* Jesus. They help give us eyes to see him, ears to hear him, and hearts to receive him. So let us stay on our toes because we can never be quite sure how or where or when he might show up next.

January 6

Silence: Stop. That's right, stop. Just sit there for a few minutes and allow yourself — body, mind, heart, and soul — to come to stillness. Stop the spinning, stop the straining, and stop the performing. Over the next few minutes there is nothing to do, nothing to achieve, and nothing to accomplish. Just be fully present. That will make your heart and soul fertile and receptive to God's word, God's voice, and God's Spirit.

Opening Prayer: Lord Jesus, help us not to miss you today. Help us to see you in whatever way(s) you choose to reveal yourself. Make us open and alert and attentive to the slightest movement of your Spirit.

Read: Matthew 2:1-11

Listen: What is God saying to you through his word today? Write about it in your journal.

Reflect: What keeps us from being able to see the beauty and the wonder that's right before our very eyes: the star in the night sky, the Child asleep in the hay, the Mystery in the midst of the mundane, the Divine contained in the ordinary?

What is it that causes us to grow hard or tired or cold or blind or deaf or indifferent to the meaning hidden in matter, to the important taken captive by the urgent? What is it that causes us to fall asleep in this life? What causes us to get so consumed with the temporal that we lose sight of the eternal? What diverts our focus away from his greater kingdom to our lesser one?

It's not something that just happens all of the sudden, but something that comes about slowly, over time. So slowly, in fact, that we don't even notice. We just look up one day and it's gone. We get lulled to sleep by the *many things* and lose sight of the *one thing*.

Respond: Who can you relate to most in the Scriptures for today? Why? What would it look like to live your life deeply aware of God and what he is up to? How will you do that?

Pray: Ask God to make your heart alive, alert, and attentive. Ask him how he is trying to reveal himself to you in ways you might not have recognized. Ask him to show you the star and the child today.

Wake us up, O God, to what really matters. We can get so distracted trying to manage our own little kingdom, that we lose sight of yours. So wake us up to you and to your movement and your presence in our lives, as well as in our world. Wake us up to who you are. Wake us up to what you are doing. Wake us up to the star and to the Child, this day and every day.

Rest: Rest in the presence of the One who sees you, knows you, and loves you.

January 7

Silence: Take a few minutes and let you heart become still and quiet. Listen to the voice of the One who calls you his beloved.

Opening Prayer: Thank you, O God, that Jesus is your beloved Son, in whom you are well pleased. And because he is your beloved child, I am as well. Help that to be the driving force behind my life and my love, for I am only able to love because you first loved me. Thank you so much for that!

Read: Matthew 3:13-17

Listen: What is God saying to you through his word today? Write about it in your journal.

Reflect: The records of the life of Jesus up to this point in the gospel are meager at best, if not downright absent. From the story of his birth, until he *comes from Galilee to the Jordan to be baptized by John,* there is only one episode recorded, and that when he is just twelve years old.

So after thirty years in virtual anonymity, what would be his introduction as he stepped into the spotlight? What was the one thing that God wanted people to know about him (and maybe even Jesus to know about himself) before he set off on this three-year journey that would end at the cross?

"This is my Son, whom I love, with him I am well-pleased." That's it. That is the one thing that God wanted everyone to know. Why? Because that's who God is; he is a lover. He loves his Son deeply, and wanted the world to know it. And he wants you and me to know the same—we are his beloved.

Did you know that you are God's beloved son or daughter? That is the thing that best defines you. It is the thing that gives you value and worth. For if you and I are beloved of God, what else do we need? It frees us up to live our lives not so that we will be loved, but because we already have been loved. Thanks be to God!

Respond: How does it make you feel to know that Jesus is God's beloved Son? How does it make you feel to know that you are his beloved child as well? Do you really believe it?

Pray: Hear the voice of the Father, proclaiming over you: "(Insert your name), you are my beloved son/daughter, in whom I am well pleased."

O God, help me to really believe that it's true.

Rest: Rest in the presence of the One who sees you, knows you, and loves you.

January 8

Silence: Take a few minutes and allow God to quiet you with his holy love. Come to rest in his loving embrace.

Opening Prayer: Lord Jesus, of course your first miracle would be at a wedding! Why should that surprise us? The bridegroom and his bride have always been one of your favorite images, probably because they're the best earthly picture we have of how deeply and intimately you love each of us. And intimacy isn't something that's broadcast, but something that's whispered, which is why only a few knew what you had really done. What a beautiful picture of who you are. Thank you for showing us.

Read: John 2:1-11

Listen: What is God saying to you through his word today? Write about it in your journal.

Reflect: *"He thus revealed his glory. . . ."* What are we to do with a God who reveals his glory in hiddenness and anonymity, except maybe try to be more like him?

It should be no surprise to anyone that the first miracle Jesus performed was at a friend's wedding and only a few people even knew about it. That tells us a lot about who Jesus is, and who he is not. I mean, who does that? Who turns water into wine and doesn't want everyone to know about it? Jesus, that's who!

Jesus, who doesn't want to take the spotlight off of the bride and groom. Jesus, who doesn't want to cause any bad light to fall on those who allowed the wine to run out in the first place. Jesus, who wants everyone to taste and enjoy the new wine of his kingdom. Jesus, who is looking forward to the day of a heavenly wedding, in which he will finally be untied with his beautiful bride, the church, for all eternity. The wine at this wedding was only a foretaste of the one to come.

Respond: What are you most drawn to in this story? Why? What does this story reveal to you about the heart of Jesus? What is his invitation to you?

Pray: Spend a few minutes in prayer, just imagining yourself at the wedding with Jesus. Take a good long look at him. Watch him as he interacts with people. What is he asking them? What is he talking about? Watch him as he enjoys the celebration. Is he laughing? Is he dancing? Is he thoroughly enjoying himself? Now watch as he speaks with the bride and groom. What is the expression on his face? What is the look in his eyes? What does all of this tell you about his heart? Finally, watch him as he tells the servants to fill the jars with water. What do you notice? How does it inspire you? Now imagine him turning to you. What does he say? What do you want to say to him?

O Jesus, thank you that you turn water into wine, not wine into water. Please do that in me today.

Rest: Rest in the presence of the One who sees you, knows you, and loves you

January 9

Silence: Silence makes space within us to encounter Jesus — to see him and hear him. Spend a few minutes quieting your soul, so that when He does show up, you will be able to see him, and when he does speak, you will be able to hear him.

Opening Prayer: We just want to see you, Lord Jesus. Once we truly see you, everything else will take care of itself.

Read: John 12:20-22

Listen: What is God saying to you through his word today? Write about it in your journal.

Reflect: It was the Passover, and people were everywhere. Typically, the city of Jerusalem would swell to six times its normal size due to people coming to worship at the temple. And they came from all over. In fact, the men who approached Philip on this particular day were Greek.

They came with one simple request: "We want to see Jesus." I suppose they figured that if they could just see him then everything else would kind of take care of itself. Their desire was as pure and simple as it was beautiful and profound.

Wouldn't it be wonderful if that was our only desire as well? Wouldn't it be incredible if that was our only request? Wouldn't it be great if all we really wanted was just to see Jesus? Oh how different our lives would be.

Respond: Where and how are you longing to see Jesus? Will you go looking for him the way these Greek men did? Will you make time and space for him? Will you be willing to be still and silent? Will you be committed to searching the Scriptures and seeking him in prayer? Will you look for him in nature and in conversations and in service?

Pray: Ask Jesus to help you see him today.

Lord Jesus, help me to see you, wherever it may be. For I can never see you unless you show yourself to me. So have mercy on me today, Lord Jesus, and help me to see you. Because if that happens, I have a suspicion that everything else in my life, and in my ministry, will take care of itself.

Rest: Rest in the presence of the One who sees you, knows you, and loves you.

January 10

Silence: Take a few minutes and allow your heart and your mind to become still and quiet. This might take a while, so be patient. Outer stillness eventually gives way to inner stillness, but it doesn't happen quickly. Give it some time; beholding Jesus cannot happen without it.

Opening Prayer: Lord Jesus, forgive me when I take the path of least resistance, when I settle for less than what you want for me because it is the easiest and most familiar thing to do. Life with you is never about settling, but always about becoming. Help me to become more like you today. Amen.

Read: John 1:10-13

Listen: What is God saying to you through his word today? Write about it in your journal.

Reflect: Beholding leads to becoming, that's the way the life of the Spirit works. When we see Jesus, when we truly see him, we will be changed. When we *behold* him, we will be transformed by the one whom we behold. We will be so captured by his life and so consumed with his love that there will be no way we can remain the same. So it stands to reason that if we have not yet been transformed, it is probably because we have not yet truly seen him. Which is not surprising, given the fact that there are so many things in this life that can cloud our vision.

It is easy to get lulled to sleep in this life. It is easy to get so busy surviving and managing and maintaining that we stop making time and space to *behold*. It is easy to get so caught up in the urgent that we forget about the important. It is easy to lose sight of the fact that the main goal of life is becoming. In the noise and chaos of daily living, it is easy to lose track of the radical nature of the gospel's call and end up *settling* for a life that is far less than the one God wants for us.

Life with Jesus is always about *becoming*, never about *settling*. Jesus doesn't want us to simply accept life as it is, but to strain toward and reach out for all that it can become. I am not talking about earning or achieving or striving, I am talking about simply becoming more and more who and what we were created to be—children of God.

There is a beautiful pattern in play here: recognize, receive, believe, and become. When we *recognize* who Jesus is and how he feels about us, and fully *receive* the gift of his great love and affection, then we will start to believe in our hearts that we are God's beloved children, which will help us to *become* all that he dreamt us to be. Our lives become an overflow of the very life of God welling up in us. That's what becoming is all about. So don't stop short of becoming; it's kind of the whole point

Respond: What word best describes your life these days, *becoming* or *surviving*? Why? What does *becoming* look like for you these days? How is God inviting you to *become*?

Pray: Ask God to show whether you are surviving or becoming. Ask him to show you who and what and how he wants you to become.

Jesus, do not let me get lulled to sleep in life. Help me to never settle for less, when you want so much more for me. Wake me up to your love and affection, so that I can be captured by it completely and, thus, become all you dreamt me to be.

Rest: Rest in the presence of the One who sees you, knows you, and loves you.

January 11

Silence: Once again we start with silence; always start with silence. Without it we have very little hope of seeing or hearing Jesus in any meaningful way.

Opening Prayer: Lord, if you are willing, you can make me clean.

Read: Luke 5:12-13

Listen: What is God saying to you through his word today? Write about it in your journal.

Reflect: I roam the countryside, fully knowing the ugliness of my affliction, fully feeling the brunt of it each moment of each day. Mine is a lonely and tortured existence. What others see on the outside is only the tip of the iceberg compared to the pain and the loneliness and the hurt and the isolation that lies within. They see the leprosy, but I see the hopelessness. They see the spots, but I see the ugliness of a heart that feels totally and completely worthless.

I alone know the depths of my self-contempt, and I am helpless to do anything about it. Oh, I've tried, but everyone and everything have failed to offer a solution for my pain. I cannot cleanse myself, so I roam about, desperately seeking healing or relief or escape or even the faintest glimmer of hope, wherever I might find it. Hope that somehow, some way, someone might help me make some sense out of this mess of a life I'm trapped inside of.

"Have mercy!" is the constant cry of my soul. Please, help! Anyone! O Jesus, Master, Son of David, can you help me? Are you willing to? Will you reach out your hand a touch my places of deepest pain and brokenness? Will you bring healing to this mess of a life? O please, Great Physician, have mercy on me and heal my affliction! For only you can offer the healing and the wholeness I so desperately need. Will you?

Respond: Julian of Norwich once wrote: "Some of us believe that God is all powerful and able to do all, and that He is all wisdom and knows how to do all. But that He is all love and will do all, there we stop. This ignorance is that which most hinders God's lovers." Do you really believe that Jesus is willing to touch you and heal you?

Pray: Ask Jesus to touch your deepest places of need. Ask him to make you whole again. Hear the love in his voice as he says, "I am willing. Be clean!" See the look in his eyes as he stretches out his hand to make you whole again. In prayer, receive his touch as he heals your broken places. Feel the full power and tenderness of his hand.

Lord Jesus, thank you that you are willing to heal me. Help me to have faith in your healing touch today, even if it ends up taking a while for me to experience the fullness of that touch.

Rest: Rest in the presence of the One who sees you, knows you, and loves you.

January 12

Silence: Hush now, O my soul, that you might be able to hear the voice of the One who calls you beloved. Be still now, that you might be touched by the One who is able to help your eyes see clearly.

Opening Prayer: Lord Jesus, thank you that you just can't seem to keep your hands off of us, but always long to touch our deepest places of brokenness and pain — not just once or twice, but always and again. Touch us again this day with your healing hands, so that we might be able to see you, and all things, clearly. Amen.

Read: Mark 8:14-26

Listen: What is God saying to you through his word today? Write about it in your journal.

Reflect: Seeing is an interesting thing. It is not something that takes place in an instant, but is a journey. Oh sure, there are times in our lives when Jesus touches our eyes and we can suddenly see like we have never seen before, but the truth is that there's always more *seeing* to be done—the seeing of things we couldn't have comprehended or appreciated at an earlier time and place. Thus, seeing is a process.

That's what Jesus was trying to help the disciples *see* as he healed this blind man: seeing often happens in stages. Therefore, he heals a man in stages right before their eyes to illustrate this.

"Do you still not *see* or understand? Are your hearts hardened? Do you have eyes but fail to *see*, and ears but fail to hear? And don't you remember? Two different times I just fed enormous groups of men and women with a couple of fish and a few loaves, and now you are worrying about having no bread? You are just like this blind man; you are seeing me in stages. Now you see dimly, but one day you will see everything clearly."

Respond: How has Jesus touched your eyes recently? How has it helped you see more clearly? How and where is your vision still blurry? How and where do you long for Jesus to touch your eyes once again?

Pray: Ask Jesus to show you where and when and how he has touched your eyes. Ask him to show you where your vision is still blurry. Ask him to touch you once again and allow you to see him, and everything else, more clearly.

O Jesus, apart from your touch I have no hope of seeing. Touch my eyes again today so I can see you, and all things, more clearly. Amen.

Rest: Rest in the presence of the One who sees you, knows you, and loves you.

January 13

Silence: "If you would just slow down and quiet your hearts, I would speak. If you would only stop your running around and wait for me, I would show myself to you. Draw near to me, O my child, and I will draw near to you."

Opening Prayer: Lord Jesus, it is so easy to lose sight of you when we are overwhelmed by our own suffering, sorrow, and pain. Yet, it is in those very times when you are mysteriously closer to us than we could ever imagine. Thank you that you are with us in the middle of our pain in ways we cannot even begin to understand, because the things that break our hearts, break your heart even more. Help us, this day, to see your heart for the pain and brokenness of this world. Amen.

Read: Mark 7:31-37

Listen: What is God saying to you through his word today? Write about it in your journal.

Reflect: Where is God in your pain? He is right in the middle of it, even if you are unable to see or comprehend it at the moment. He is not absent, he is not indifferent, and he is not distant. In fact, he is intensely and intimately present. That is because your pain causes him pain. He groans over your suffering and sorrow, just like he did with the man who was deaf and mute. Jesus could not stay away from those who were broken and hurting. In fact, those are the people he was most drawn to, because those are the ones he came to heal. And he could not keep is hands from the places of deepest brokenness and pain in their lives. And in this man's case, he could not keep from putting his *fingers in his ears,* or *spitting and touching his tongue.* That's just the kind of God he is.

He is near. He is present. He is involved. He wants you to know that your heartbreak breaks his heart even more. Because the life he created you for was never intended to be filled with brokenness and pain. Allow his hands to touch your deepest places of woundedness today and make you whole.

Respond: How do you think Jesus feels about your pain? Where in your life do you long for his touch? What do you think he might be up to in your life these days?

Pray: Ask God to allow you to hear his groan. Ask him to show you what is making him groan in and for you. Ask him to touch you in your places of deepest pain and brokenness, and to begin to make those places whole again.

Lord Jesus, help us to hear your groan, and let it show us more about your heart. Help us to learn to groan with you over the things are not what they were intended to be. And as you touch us and heal us, Lord Jesus, help us to be your healing hands in the lives of those who are groaning deeply right now.

Rest: Rest in the presence of the One who sees you, knows you, and loves you.

January 14

Silence: Sometimes we are actually afraid of silence; it says too much. While silence may be a scary place, it is also the place of deep encounter with God, so we must learn to gather up our courage and allow our souls to become still and quiet before God today. It will make room within us for him to speak.

Opening Prayer: Lord Jesus, we long to see your glory, but sometimes our own struggles blind us and get in the way. Help us, this day, to get past the struggle, so that we might be able to see you, even in the midst of our pain and doubts and questions.

Read: John 11:17-44

Listen: What is God saying to you through his word today? Write about it in your journal.

Reflect: In times of deep sorrow, we stand with Martha and Mary in grief and despair, confused as to how anything good could possibly come out of *this*. Asking ourselves, as they did, "Where is God? Does he not care? Could he not have stopped *this* from happening?"

That's when we hear the voice of Jesus as he tenderly says, both to them and to us, "Didn't I tell you that if you believed, you would see the glory of God? In spite of the pain, in spite of the brokenness, in spite of the waves and waves of sadness and sorrow, I am still at work. And one day, if you believe, you will see the glory of God."

At moments like these it is so hard to process, much less believe. All there is now is pain—lots and lots of pain. So much pain that it takes up all of the room within us. Thus, there are times in this life when the only thing we can see is our own pain.

Who could ever imagine that God would be big enough to work through something like *this*? Who could ever dream that we would be able to see the glory of God rise up out of the ashes of such bitter grief and sorrow and sadness?

And then we *behold* a weeping Jesus. Not only does he care enough to weep for our pain, but he also cares enough to redeem it. Death is not an end, but a beginning. It is merely a doorway into a deeper, fuller, richer, and truer life.

So he stands with us in the midst of the darkness and despair. He tells us to roll away the stone of our doubt and our anger and our disbelief. He tells us to watch as he brings life out of the cold, dark tomb. And he invites us to join him as he brings joy out of sorrow, victory out of defeat, and hope out of despair.

Respond: Where is God in the midst of your pain? What does that tell you about what you really believe to be true about him? Where is God saying to you, "Did I not tell you that if you believed, you would see the glory of God?" What is your response?

Pray: Give Jesus your pain and your brokenness and your sorrow and your questions today in prayer. Listen as he speaks the words: "Did I not tell you that if you believed, you would see the glory of God?"

Help us to see your glory today, Lord Jesus, in spite of the all the darkness and sadness and despair.

Rest: Rest in the presence of the One who sees you, knows you, and loves you.

January 15

Silence: Take a few minutes to be still and quiet. Don't be surprised or alarmed if this is difficult to do; it takes a while. It does not happen immediately. All of the voices around you and within you will take some time to stop their clamoring and come to rest, but they will…eventually. Just give it some time. Once you have a sense of stillness, read the opening prayer. Now your soul is in a better state to interact with God.

Opening Prayer: Thank you, Lord Jesus, that there is always more to you than meets the eye. You are always bigger and more beautiful and more glorious than we could ever see or imagine. Thank you for those moments in life when you pull back the curtain a little bit and give us a glimpse of who you really are.

Read: Matthew 17:1-9

Listen: What is God saying to you through his word today? Write about it in your journal.

Reflect: We tend to see God through the lenses of our own preferences. Which means that oftentimes we don't really see him at all, we just see our own projections of him. As the French philosopher Voltaire once said, "God made man in his image and man returned the favor."

That's why from time to time God has to get our attention. He has to open our eyes to who he really is and what he is really like. These are what I like to refer to as the "wow moments" in life. They are moments when our eyes are opened and we are able to see things as they really are—in all of their beauty and all of their majesty.

They are transcendent moments. Moments that leave us speechless and breathless. Moments that leave us with our mouths open and our hearts overwhelmed. Moments that connect us with the knowledge of something (or Someone) so much bigger and more beautiful and more glorious than we ever imagined.

Moments when God leads us out of the valley and takes us up to the mountaintop where the air is fresher and our vision clearer. Moments when God pulls back the thin veil that separates time from eternity and gives us a little glimpse of his infinite glory. Moments when God breaks out of the tiny little boxes we have put him in and shows us that he cannot and will not be tamed or contained. Moments that show us that there is so much more to him that we can ever fully know.

These are the moments that transform us. Will you join him on the mountaintop today?

Respond: What does Jesus want to show you about himself today? What new vision of himself does he want to give you? How does he want you to see his glory?

Pray: Join Jesus on the mountaintop today in prayer. What do you see? What do you hear? What curtain does he want to pull back? What does he want to show you about himself? What is your response?

Lord Jesus, show us your glory. Help us to see you as you really are.

Rest: Rest in the presence of the One who sees you, knows you, and loves you.

January 16

Silence: Silence is the place of genuine transformation. It is the place where we stand face to face with Jesus — open, naked, and vulnerable. No props to get in the way, no things to run off and do, nothing and no one to hide behind. Sit silently before God today and allow him the time and the space to touch and transform you.

Opening Prayer: Lord Jesus, free us from the addiction of busyness. Help us to never love the things we do for God, more than we love the God we do them for.

Read: Mark 9:2

Listen: What is God saying to you through his word today? Write about it in your journal.

Reflect: *"After six days Jesus took Peter, James, and John with him and led them up a high mountain, where they were all alone. There he was transfigured before them."* (Mark 9:2)

Nowadays, it seems like the biggest enemy of encountering Jesus, and seeing his glory, is incessant busyness. Sadly, this is particularly true of those in ministry. And why not? After all, we are working for kingdom purposes here, right? Well, maybe. And maybe not. Sometimes our unbridled busyness has more to do with us—our egos, our need to be needed, our perceived indispensability, and our insecurity—than it does with Jesus.

The problem is that if we never encounter Jesus ourselves, how can we ever hope that those under our care will? We must relentlessly make time and space in our lives for ongoing encounter with Jesus. But the sad truth is that all too often we fail to see the glory of Jesus simply because we are too busy to follow him up the mountain.

Respond: How is busyness affecting your life right now? How do you try to rationalize it? How does it keep you from seeing the glory of Jesus? How has he revealed his glory to you lately? What did it do in your heart, soul, and life?

Pray: Follow Jesus up the mountain today in prayer. Watch him as he is transfigured before you. Behold his glory. Be enveloped by the cloud of God's presence, power, and love. Hear his voice as he proclaims: "This is my Son, whom I love. Listen to him!" What do you want to say to Jesus as a result?

Lord Jesus, help us to never be too busy to follow you up the mountain, so that we can see your glory. Amen.

Rest: Rest in the presence of the One who sees you, knows you, and loves you.

January 17

Silence: Settle yourself in solitude and you will come upon Him in yourself. ~Teresa of Avila

Opening Prayer: Forgive me, Lord Jesus, for all of the ways I think I can see, when I am still blind. Open my eyes to my own blindness and help me to see you, myself, and others as they really are.

Read: John 9:1-41

Listen: What is God saying to you through his word today? Write about it in your journal.

Reflect: There are basically three different types of people in this world: those who can see, those who can't see, and those who can't see but think they can. Here in John 9, Jesus heals a man in the second category, in order to try and help those in the third category understand that they are blind, just in a whole different way.

I mean, being blind is bad enough, right? But being blind and thinking you can see, that's far worse. It's impossible to help someone like that because they do not think there's a problem in the first place. And the realization that there's a problem is a significant part of finding the solution. The blind man must first realize he's blind before he can ever have any real appreciation for being able to see.

The funny thing is that most of us think we see just fine, which makes us totally oblivious to all of the ways we are still unable to do so. How can a blind man see his blind spots? He can't!

The moral of the story is that we are all in need of grace. We are all in need of having Jesus come to us and touch our eyes over and over again, so that we might finally be able to see the way he sees. That's the only way we will not be blind.

Respond: What stands out to you in the story of the blind man? Why? How has God touched your eyes and helped you to see? Where might you still be blind, or have blind spots?

Pray: Ask Jesus to touch your eyes. Ask him to show you the ways and the places you are still blind. Listen to his response.

Lord Jesus, I cannot see unless you touch my eyes. Help me to see like you see. Amen.

Rest: Rest in the presence of the One who sees you, knows you, and loves you.

January 18

Silence: Spend a few minutes in silence, stilling and quieting your soul, like a weaned child with its mother. This will help you be open and receptive to all that God wants to do in you today.

Opening Prayer: Thank you, Lord Jesus, that you are the light of the world and when we walk with you we walk in the light of truth. Therefore, help us to do just that. Help us to never live in the shadows, trying to make people think that we are better than we really are. Help us, instead, to live openly and honestly before you and each other—never covering or posturing or pretending. Just give us the courage and the grace and the strength to live authentically. That way everyone will know that any good they see is only because of you.

Read: John 3:21

Listen: What is God saying to you through his word today? Write about it in your journal.

Reflect: Living in the light means walking in the light of truth. It means leaving behind all that is dark and hidden and false. It involves not trying to make people think I am better than I am. If I can somehow resist the tendency to hide my warts, my wounds, and my deficiencies, then I can live a life that truly reveals God's power and his love. I can live a life that glorifies him, rather than one that glorifies myself. In which case, my inadequacies would highlight his adequacy, my weaknesses would highlight his strength, and my deficiencies would highlight his sufficiency.

Lord Jesus, help me to live in the light of your truth, so that everyone can see that the only good in me is because of who you are.

Respond: What does it meant to walk in the light of truth? How is God inviting you to do that? What does that look like?

Pray: Ask Jesus to shine his light on you. Ask him for the courage and the strength and the grace to live in that light. Ask him to show you where you are still living in darkness and invite him into that.

Shine your light, Lord Jesus, into our dark places, so that everyone can see the truth about us and about you. Amen.

Rest: Rest in the presence of the One who sees you, knows you, and loves you.

January 19

Silence: Hasten unto Him who calls you in the silences of your heart. ~Thomas R. Kelly

Opening Prayer: Help me, Lord Jesus, to know that when storms come, it does not mean that you have abandoned me. It just means that I have to keep my eyes open for how and where and when you will come to me in the midst of them.

Read: Matthew 14:22-24

Listen: What is God saying to you through his word today? Write about it in your journal.

Reflect: Sometimes it takes a storm. Maybe that's why Jesus *made* the disciples get into the boat and go on ahead of him. (Mt.14:22) It's eerily similar to what happened a few chapters earlier (Mt. 8:23-27), except this time he was not asleep in the bow, but was nowhere to be found. Would they still be able to trust him, even when they could not see him? Could they trust his heart, even when they could not see his hand?

The fact is, Jesus knew exactly what he was doing. He was about to grow their faith exponentially, and faith rarely grows without a little chaos. Jesus was willing to do whatever it took to capture their hearts and to grow their faith. He knew full well the intensity of the storm that was awaiting them, but he also knew full well how profoundly he was going to meet them in the midst of it.

He did not cause the storm; it was simply the result of living in a fallen world. In this life, storms are going to come; they are inevitable. But it was not the *storm* part that Jesus was really interested in, but the *coming to them* in the midst of it part. He wanted them to know his grace and his power and his love and his provision in ways they could only know by having gone through it.

And it is the same for each of us. Aren't you glad that Jesus isn't willing to let you settle for less, when he wants so much more for you? Even if it takes a storm to get you there. Are you willing to trust him?

Respond: What are the storms in your life these days? How are they inviting you to trust Jesus in a new and deeper way?

Pray: Look for Jesus in the midst of your storm; you never know how or where or when he might show up. He *will*, however, show up.

Help me to trust you, Lord Jesus, in the midst of my storms. Help me to be able to trust your heart, even when I can't see your hand.

Rest: Rest in the presence of the One who sees you, knows you, and loves you.

January 20

Silence: Until you can put aside the noise and the clamor and the busyness, it is unlikely that you will be able to hear from God in any meaningful way. Until you can leave the crowds behind and quiet your heart and soul, it will be difficult to hear the voice of the One who often speaks in a gentle whisper. Still your mind and quiet your soul, so that you might be able to hear from him today.

Opening Prayer: Thank you, Lord Jesus, that you did not allow the demands and agendas of others to determine what you did, and what you did not do. Thank you that you often dismissed the crowds so you could simply be with your Father in prayer. Help us to have the courage to do the same. Amen.

Read: Matthew 14:23

Listen: What is God saying to you through his word today? Write about it in your journal.

Reflect:

> i love that Jesus
> never seemed to
> have any trouble
> leaving the crowds behind
> in order to pray
> i wish i could say the same

Respond: What effect do the crowds have on you? What effect do you think Jesus wants them to have? Are you able to leave them behind in order to spend time with your Heavenly Father? Will you?

Pray: Be still and quiet before God. Just spend some time being with him. Is that a difficult thing for you to do? If so, ask God why that is? Ask him to show you what effect the crowds have on you. Listen for his response.

Lord Jesus, help me to be like you. Help me to leave the crowds behind and spend time with my Father. Amen.

Rest: Rest in the presence of the One who sees you, knows you, and loves you.

January 21

Silence: It takes a while for the waters of your heart and soul to become still and calm. And it is only when they are still and calm that you can see what's underneath. Take a few minutes as we begin to allow the waters of your soul to come to stillness. That will enable you to see and to hear God more clearly.

Opening Prayer: Lord Jesus, thank you that you are *the God who comes*, even in times of chaos and turmoil. Help us to have eyes to see you and ears to hear you, regardless of whatever might be going on around us or within us. Amen.

Read: Matthew 14:25

Listen: What is God saying to you through his word today? Write about it in your journal.

Reflect: Why the fourth watch? Why did Jesus wait so long to go out to them? After all, they had been out on the lake all night, *buffeted by the wind and the waves* for as many as twelve hours. Why not go out to them sooner? Why wait until they were bruised, battered, and beaten?

Have you ever asked that question? Have you ever wondered why God seems to let the storms of life go on for so long before he eventually shows up in the midst of them? Is he testing our faith? Is he trying to see if we really believe he is willing and able to calm the storm? Because believing that he *can* and believing that he *will* are two totally different things.

In all honesty, over the course of my life I have found Jesus to be a fourth-watch-kind-of-God. In my experience, he tends to wait a while before he *comes out to us*. And even when he does come out to us, sometimes our circumstances are so chaotic that we cannot recognize him.

The fourth watch is the point in time when we've reached the end of our ropes; when we just can't do it anymore. It's that moment when we realize we're all rowed out. The fourth watch is when we finally cry, "Uncle!" When we finally say, "I've got nothing left in the tank." It's the point in time when we've been brought to a place of total desperation and absolute dependence, when we have finally come to the end of ourselves. Sadly, for most of us, that is a really long journey.

The fourth watch is also the time when God says: "I want you to trust me. Not me *and* your own efforts, not me *and* your own giftedness, not me *and* favorable circumstances, not even me *and* your friends and family, but me *alone*. And you will never learn to trust me *alone* until all of the other things have been stripped away and there is nothing left to cling to. That's when I finally have you where I want you. That's when true growth and transformation can finally take place. That's when you reach the point where you can become all that I dreamt you to be."

So, I suppose if it takes until the *fourth watch* to get me there, then it's worth it, right?

Respond: Where and how does it feel like you are in the fourth watch? How do you think God feels about that? What do you think he's up to?

Pray: Ask God for eyes to see him and ears to hear him in all the circumstances of your life. Ask him to show you what he's up to in the areas that are messy and broken and chaotic. Ask him for peace and patience and trust in the midst of it.

Lord Jesus, help me to know that when you wait until the fourth watch to come out to me, you are not just being difficult. You are trying to accomplish something very good in me. Help me to never let the storms of this life, or the timing of your coming, make me doubt the goodness of your heart.

Rest: Rest in the presence of the One who sees you, knows you, and loves you.

January 22

Silence: The voices in our heads and our hearts are loud indeed. So loud, in fact, that they have a tendency to drown out all the other voices, particularly the still, small voice of God. Take a few minutes of silence and allow those voices to quiet down; it will make it much more likely that when God does finally speak, you will be able to hear him.

Opening Prayer: Lord Jesus, help me to realize that the storms and chaos of this life can keep me from seeing and recognizing you. They can even cause me to make up narratives about myself and others that are simply not true. Help me, Lord Jesus, to live in your truth, because it is your truth that sets me free. Amen.

Read: Matthew 14:26-27

Listen: What is God saying to you through his word today? Write about it in your journal.

Reflect: So the disciples had convinced themselves that Jesus was a ghost. Interesting. They had created a story in their minds that was not even true. Circumstances clouded their vision, producing fear and keeping them from being able to recognize that it was actually Jesus who was standing out there on the sea. I wonder how often that is the case for each of us?

I wonder how often we allow our interpretation of situations and circumstances to create a narrative that simply doesn't exist. I wonder how often we make up stories for ourselves and others that are only the creation of our own fearful minds and insecure hearts. Sin has made us, like the disciples, prone to misinterpretation. We create stories for ourselves and for others that are just not true. In other words, because of sin we have become unreliable narrators, even of our own stories. Sin has kept us from being able to see clearly.

Which makes me ask, what is the story I am telling myself right now? And is it even true? Where have I convinced myself that something is true, when it is really not? Where have I allowed circumstances to keep me from recognizing Jesus?

Respond: Where have you created a story (for yourself or for others) that is not really true? What is that story? What is the truth? Where and how have circumstances kept you from being able to recognize Jesus?

Pray: Ask God to show you those stories you have created for yourself and others that are just not true. Ask him to allow his truth to set you free.

Lord Jesus, give me the eyes to see you (and your truth) clearly, even in the midst of the storms and the chaos.

Rest: Rest in the presence of the One who sees you, knows you, and loves you.

January 23

Silence: Take a few minutes and become still and quiet. Allow your heart and soul to come to rest in the presence of your God.

Opening Prayer: Lord Jesus, reach out your hand and take hold of me this day. Draw me near to your heart and fill me with your life and your love. Amen.

Read: Matthew 14:28-29

Listen: What is God saying to you through his word today? Write about it in your journal.

Reflect: The space *in between* is holy ground, because it is the place of complete trust and absolute dependence. It is the space between the boat and Jesus, between letting go and being taken hold of, between departure and arrival. It is the place of genuine transformation, because it produces some of the most fertile soil for Jesus to grow his life within us.

The saints call it liminal space. A *limen* is an entrance or doorway. Thus, it is a passageway from one place to another that ushers in a new beginning, a new way of being. It is the space where we have given up control and agenda, and have placed ourselves in the loving care of our Savior. We are at his mercy to do with us what he will.

The problem is that not many of us are willing to go there. Not many hear the call of Jesus to "come" and are willing to leave the comfort and safety of the boat in order to experience life with him on the high seas. Simon Peter was willing to take that step, and in return he received the privilege of walking with Jesus on the water. I'll bet it was a decision he never regretted.

Respond: How are you living *in between* right now? What fruit is it producing in you? How is it nurturing your life with Jesus?

Pray: Ask God to show you how he is calling you to live *in between*. Ask him what he's trying to accomplish in you as a result. Ask him to show you the fruit of that space.

Lord Jesus, you know how uncomfortable I am living *in between*, but that is the life you have called me to. Show me, therefore, how to flourish in it. Show me what you are growing in me as a result. And help me to be content living in that space until you reach out your hand and take hold of me.

Rest: Rest in the presence of the One who sees you, knows you, and loves you.

January 24

Silence: Start with silence. It always starts with silence. It's an ancient dance: first there is silence, then God speaks, and then things come into being. From the first page of the Scriptures it is a recurring pattern. It's God's way, so start with silence today.

Opening Prayer: Lord Jesus, thank you that you always invite me to come. It is not, however, an invitation for the faint of heart, so give me the strength and the courage and the grace to give up control, to leave the security and familiarity of the boat behind, and to step out onto the sea with you. That is where I will truly experience your life and your power. Amen.

Read: Matthew 14:29

Listen: What is God saying to you through his word today? Write about it in your journal.

Reflect: There are no two ways about it, *stepping down out of the boat* takes courage, especially if you have no idea exactly what you are stepping into. But it is also incredibly exciting, because it is an invitation to a new way of being and of seeing.

It is *a leaving behind* of the old and tired and worn, but also a leaving behind of what's safe and familiar and comfortable. It's like you are being asked to let go of the trapeze bar that is currently in your hands, in order to grab hold of a new one that has not yet appeared. It is as terrifying as it is invigorating, just ask Simon Peter.

This is the life Jesus calls us to: stepping *down* and *out*. It is a life of wonderfully frightening dependence on him. A life where we must learn to trust simply by trusting, by stepping out into the unknown without the old handholds we have gotten so used to. By stepping out onto the wild and untamed sea, before we really know if the sea will hold us. That is the life into which Jesus says, "Come." The only question is: Will we?

Respond: What is Jesus inviting you into these days? What does stepping down out of the boat look like for you right now? Will you do it?

Pray: Ask God what "stepping down out of the boat" looks like for you right now. Ask him for the strength and the courage and the grace to do it.

Lord Jesus, help me to follow you wherever you may lead, and help me to do whatever you may ask me to do.

Rest: Rest in the presence of the One who sees you, knows you, and loves you.

January 25

Silence: There is no shame in silence, because silence makes us attentive to God. What shame could there possibly be in that? It would, however, be a shame if we ever got too busy to be silent. Spend a few minutes in silence, preparing your heart for whatever God might have for you today.

Opening Prayer: Lord Jesus, when the storms come and the winds are blowing, when the waves threaten to sweep me away, help me to keep my eyes focused on you and not on the chaos that is going on within or around me.

Read: Matthew 14:30

Listen: What is God saying to you through his word today? Write about it in your journal.

Reflect: *"But when he saw the wind, he was afraid, and beginning to sink. He cried out, 'Lord, save me.'"* (Matthew 14:30)

You were doing great, what happened? Why did you allow your surroundings to determine the state of your heart? Why did you let your fear overpower your faith? Did you not think I would take care of you?

I know the wind is strong, but I am stronger. I know the waves are big, but I am bigger. Do not be afraid. Do not let fear make you its puppet. Chaos does not have the final word, peace does. Fear does not have ultimate control, love does. So do not let fear have free reign over you.

Just keep your eyes focused on me, my child, and all will be well. Cast all of your fears and cares on me, for I love you.

Respond: Where is fear getting the better of you these days? How are you allowing circumstances to determine your life? What does it look like to keep your eyes focused on Jesus?

Pray: Listen to the call of Jesus to "Come." What does that mean? What does that look like? What is he inviting you to? Ask him to help you not succumb to fear, but to keep your eyes focused on him.

Here I come, Jesus. Take care of me and give me faith.

Rest: Rest in the presence of the One who sees you, knows you, and loves you.

January 26

Silence: Silence is nothing else but waiting for God's Word and coming from God's Word with a blessing. ~Dietrich Bonhoeffer

Opening Prayer: "Fear not, for I have redeemed you; I have called you by name; you are mine. When you pass through the waters, I will be with you; and when you pass through the waters, they will not sweep over you. When you walk through the fire, you will not be burned; the flames will not set you ablaze. For I am the Lord, your God, the Holy One of Israel, your Savior." (Isaiah 43:1-3)

Read: Matthew 14:31

Listen: What is God saying to you through his word today? Write about it in your journal.

Reflect: *O you of little faith, why did you doubt?* I've got you. Do not fear when the waves are large and the wind is strong, and you have lost the nerve to face it all. Do not be dismayed when your eyes wander and become so focused on your circumstances and surroundings that you lose sight of your Savior. Do not be filled with doubt when your heart gets so overwhelmed that your faith fails and you find yourself beginning to sink. I am with you. Just call out my name and I will take hold of you. You can always count on me.

Respond: Where and how have fear and doubt caused you to lose faith in the Savior? Do you really believe he's got you?

Pray: Give God those situations and circumstances in your life that are causing you fear, doubt, and insecurity. Imagine him reaching out his strong and loving hand in the midst of them and taking hold of you.

Lord Jesus, forgive me when my doubt overwhelms my faith. Help me to truly believe that you've got me, no matter what.

Rest: Rest in the presence of the One who sees you, knows you, and loves you.

January 27

Silence: Allow the One who stilled the wind and the waves to still the chaos and turbulence of your heart right now.

Opening Prayer: Lord Jesus, truly you are the Son of God.

Read: Matthew 14:32-33

Listen: What is God saying to you through his word today? Write about it in your journal.

Reflect: *"And those in the boat worshipped him, saying, 'Truly you are the Son of God.'" (Matthew 14:33)*

There are moments in life when we realize that we are in the presence of something, or Someone, much larger than ourselves. Moments when our jaws drop in wonder and delight, and our knees bow in humility and awe. Moments when the only word we are able to utter is, "Wow!"

These are moments of transcendence, moments when the curtain is pulled back just a little and we are able to see things as they really are. The fog lifts, or the waves are stilled, and we are able to clearly see the power and the glory of the One who called all things into being.

These moments change us, because they help us to see in a new way. They help put everything in perspective. They make our own little lives and our own little problems seem so small and inconsequential in the grand scheme of things. Eternity has broken into our world and reminded us of the way things were intended to be. It has reminded us that we are only a small part of a great big story.

Respond: When was the last time God moved in a way that left you saying, "Wow!"? What did that experience do within you? What does it still do within you? How does God want to *wow* you today? When was the last time you responded, "Truly you are the Son of God"?

Pray: Ask God to help you to recognize the transcendence going on all around you. Ask him to *wow* you with his love, his power, and his presence.

Truly, Lord Jesus, you are the Son of God!

Rest: Rest in the presence of the One who sees you, knows you, and loves you.

January 28

Silence: Take a few minutes to become still and quiet. Shut your mouth, open your ears, and make room for God to speak.

Opening Prayer: Lord Jesus, help me to see you, really see you, as I look into the Scriptures today. Help me to see your face, help me to hear your voice, and help me to experience your touch. I long for you, Lord Jesus, so please reveal yourself to me through your Word and your Spirit this day. Amen.

Read: John 4:1-6

Listen: What is God saying to you through his word today? Write about it in your journal.

Reflect: Why did Jesus *have to go through Samaria*? It was not for geographic reasons, though Samaria stood right between Judea and Galilee. Any God-fearing Jew would have gone around, and yet Jesus chose to go through. Why?

He went through because there was someone there who would never have come to him, so he went to her. Someone who was in desperate need of an encounter with the Living God. Jesus was the initiator. Jesus was the pursuer. That's just who Jesus is. He is the God who *comes*; it's just his nature. He is the one who is always coming after us, always initiating, always pursuing. Ultimately, Jesus is a lover in relentless pursuit of his beloved, even to this very day.

So why did Jesus *have to* go through Samaria? He had to go through Samaria because he just couldn't stay away, his heart wouldn't allow it. He couldn't stay away from the woman at the well, and he can't stay away from you and me. In fact, he is pursuing you at this very moment. He has something he wants to say to you, something he wants you to see, something he wants you to know. The only question is: When he speaks, will you be listening? When he comes, will you be paying attention?

Respond: Do you see Jesus as a pursuer? How is he pursuing you these days?

Pray: Ask God to show you the ways he is (and has been) pursuing you. Listen for his response.

Lord Jesus, thank you that you *had to* go through Samaria, and thank you that you *have to* come after me. Thank you that you are a pursuer, it's simply who you are. I am so grateful for that.

Rest: Rest in the presence of the One who sees you, knows you, and loves you.

January 29

Silence: Still your body, quiet your mind, and calm your heart. Take a few deep breaths. Relax. Let go of whatever may be causing you stress, tension, or anxiety. Just sit here for a minute or two and be present. Let go of whatever you may be dragging into this time, it will only keep you from being able to hear Jesus.

Opening Prayer: Lord Jesus, thank you that you were both tired and thirsty. Thus, you can understand me in ways that I can't even imagine. Give me the gift of your living water this day, so that I might experience the life and the love you created me for.

Read: John 4:7-10

Listen: What is God saying to you through his word today? Write about it in your journal.

Reflect: Jesus was tired and thirsty. I don't know about you, but I think there is something beautifully mysterious and incredibly wonderful about that. I mean, why in the world would the God of all creation put himself in a position where he was both tired and thirsty? Unless, of course, it was to show us that he knows exactly how we feel.

He was intimately familiar with the plight of the woman who stood before him that day. He knew her thirst, he knew her weariness, and he knew her deepest longings, because he had experienced each of them firsthand.

"You're thirsty, aren't you? Yeah, me too. And tired too? I totally get that. And not only is your body tired and thirsty, but your soul is as well. I can actually take care of that. I can give you water that's qualitatively different from any water you have ever tasted before, because the water I give you is not for your body, but for your soul."

Only someone who knew that thirst could talk about it is such a thoughtful and alluring way. In a way that drew this woman further and further into the truth and the fullness and the life he was trying to help her discover and experience for herself.

And he knows you too. He knows your thirst, he knows your weariness, he knows your deepest longings, and he wants you to experience the fullness and the life he created you for. All you have to do is come and drink.

Respond: How does it make you feel to know that Jesus was tired and thirsty? Do you really think that Jesus understands your thirst and can satisfy it? What does it look like to drink his living water?

Pray: Are you tired and thirsty? What is making you that way? Tell Jesus about it and listen to his reply.

Jesus, thank you that you were tired and thirsty, because I'm tired and thirsty too. You know exactly how I feel and are wonderfully able to give me the rest and the satisfaction I most deeply long for. Give me the fullness and the life that I was created for.

Rest: Rest in the presence of the One who sees you, knows you, and loves you.

January 30

Silence: It is in silence that the soul learns to listen; it is in stillness that the eyes learn to see. Therefore, be still and silent before the Lord today.

Opening Prayer: O Jesus, that living water you talk about sounds so great, but I don't really know how to access it. My rope won't reach to the bottom of the well. Give me your living water this day, and then show me how to drink it.

Read: John 4:11-15

Listen: What is God saying to you through his word today? Write about it in your journal.

Reflect: Contrary to popular opinion, God doesn't want to become a part of our lives, he wants us to become a part of his. That's what he was trying to tell the woman he met at the well that day. Thus, life with God is mostly about learning how to cultivate and nurture the life of God within us. His life within us is the mysterious *living water* he keeps talking about. It is the only water that can truly satisfy and leave us where we are never thirsty again.

It is not something that can be forced, manufactured, or contrived, but only something that can be received. It is a gift, something that God gives us. Our main job is to simply open ourselves up to its flow and then learn how to drink, which takes practice. Practice in making space and time for God, practice in reading the Scriptures and praying the prayers, and practice in being still and silent.

It takes an awareness and an attentiveness to the stirrings of the Spirit within us. It takes a desire to engage in the intimacy and the passion of the life that is being offered us. It takes turning away from all of the *broken wells* we tend to drink from (Jer. 2:13) and turning back to Jesus, the *well of living water*.

Respond: How do you attempt to taste the living water of Jesus? How do you nurture the life of God within you? Is it bringing life and fullness to your soul? Why, or why not?

Pray: Ask Jesus to give you his living water today. Take a sip. Taste and see that he is good.

Jesus, teach me how to drink your living water, so that I can have the fullness and the life and the love you created me for.

Rest: Rest in the presence of the One who sees you, knows you, and loves you.

January 31

Silence: Don't skip this part. Sit in silence for a few minutes and allow your heart and mind to come to stillness. This is a very important part of the process. Give God your full attention, so that you do not miss whatever it is that he has for you today.

Opening Prayer: Lord Jesus, you made me for your love and nothing short of that love will ever truly satisfy. Forgive me when I allow poor substitutes to take the place of the real thing.

Read: John 4:16-18

Listen: What is God saying to you through his word today? Write about it in your journal.

Reflect: *"You are right when you say you have no husband. The fact is, you have had five husbands, and the man you have right now is not your husband. What you have said is quite true."* John 4:17-18)

What was the look in the eyes of the Savior as he uttered these words to this lost and thirsty woman? Was it a look of disdain, judgment, and disgust? Or was it a look of compassion, longing, and tenderness? How you answer that question will tell you so much about what you really believe to be true about God. And that is really significant.

If we are consistent with the Jesus we see in the rest of the Gospels, I think it must've been a look of love. Jesus didn't ever look at the lost and broken with disdain, but with love and delight, with compassion and desire, with acceptance and invitation.

Thus, he did not say these words to shame her, but to awaken her. It was his way of saying, "You have not yet found your beloved. He is the one standing right in front of you." Because more than anything else, the story of God is the story of a lover in constant pursuit of his beloved. Do you believe that? Do you believe it for this woman? Do you believe it for yourself?

What do you think the eyes of Jesus hold as they look at you today? How could it be anything other than love?

Respond: How do you think God really sees you? How is God trying to awaken you to his love? What keeps getting in the way?

Pray: Look into the eyes of Jesus today in prayer. What do you see? What does that do within you?

Lord Jesus, forgive us when we believe that you look at us through the eyes of criticism or anger or disgust. Help us to see ourselves as you see us — as your beloved. Only then can we see others that way as well.

Rest: Rest in the presence of the One who sees you, knows you, and loves you.

February 1

Silence: "In repentance and rest is your salvation, in quietness and trust is your strength." (Is. 30:15) Be still and quiet before the Lord. Make space within you to see him and hear him.

Opening Prayer: Lord Jesus, you want all of my attention and affection, not just part of it. And I can only learn to rightly love others, if I love you above and before all else. Help me to do so.

Read: John 4:19-24

Listen: What is God saying to you through his word today? Write about it in your journal.

Reflect: Birds have a habit of building their nests in the wreath on our front door. Which is all well and good until we open the door too quickly one day, and before we know it we have a bird in our house.

The last time this happened I was at a bit of a loss as to how to get the bird out of the house without harming it. Our entryway is quite tall and even with a ladder we could never reach high enough to be able to capture the bird safely.

Luckily, my wife came to the rescue. She grabbed a soft blanket, went upstairs to the balcony that overlooks our entryway, and threw the blanket over the top of the bird, capturing it safely so that we could release it back into the great outdoors.

I'm sure as soon as the blanket made contact with the bird, she (the bird) thought that she was doomed. Little did she know that *sometimes you have to be captured in order to be set free*. Which is true for birds and true for us.

It is not until we are captured — seized by the power of the Great Affection — that we can actually begin to live as free men and women. We must be captured by God's unfailing love before we will ever be free to love him, and others, the way he desires us to. It was the pull of his love that transformed the woman at the well, and it is the pull of his love that transforms each of us. Until we are captured by a Greater Love, we will always be held captive by lesser ones.

Respond: What are you most captured by these days? How have you been seized by the power of the Great Affection lately? What effect has that had on your life?

Pray: Ask Jesus to show you what is keeping you from experiencing the freedom of being fully captured by his love. Listen for his response.

Lord Jesus, nothing stands in the way of your love for me, help me to make sure that nothing stands in the way of my love for you.

Rest: Rest in the presence of the One who sees you, knows you, and loves you.

February 2

Silence: Stop me from my busy spinning, O Lord, and help my heart and soul to come to rest in you this day. (*Selah*)

Opening Prayer: Lord Jesus, we look for answers, we look for hope, and we look for peace. We ask, "Who is the one who loves me like I most deeply desire to be loved?" And even before we have fully asked the question, you say to us, "I AM." Help us to believe it's true, for only in you, the great I AM, will we find the love and the life and the fullness we are looking for. Amen.

Read: John 4:25-26

Listen: What is God saying to you through his word today? Write about it in your journal.

Reflect: I AM the One, my beloved. I am the one you have been waiting for and yearning for and hoping for. I am the one who loves you the way you long to be loved. I am the one who can deliver you from all of your addictions and imperfections and dysfunctions. I am the one who can transform your mundane existence into something beautiful and extraordinary and full. I am the one who can awaken you to the life and the love you most deeply desire. I am the one who can satisfy your every thirst, so come, my beloved, come and drink. I made you for fullness, so leave those other loves behind; you will not need them anymore.

Respond: What does I AM really mean to you today? Who or what do you need him to be?

Pray: Ask God to help you truly believe that he is *the One* — the one you want, the one you need, the one you have been looking for, the one who loves you, the one who gives you life.

Thank you, Lord Jesus, that you are the One. You are the one we've been looking for and longing for and hoping for all of our lives.

Rest: Rest in the presence of the One who sees you, knows you, and loves you.

February 3

Silence: Hush, my soul, pay no attention to all of the voices and distractions within you. If you will just be still and quiet, they will eventually stop their clamoring. If you will go into your closet and shut the door, they will eventually stop knocking and go away. But if you continue to answer their call, you will not have one moment of rest or peace. You will be unable to hear your God when he speaks. So, hush now, my soul, pay no attention to all of the voices and distractions within you.

Opening Prayer: Thank you, Lord Jesus, that we, like the woman at the well, do not need our water jars anymore. We can toss them aside because you offer to fill our hearts and our lives to overflowing with your unending life and your unfailing love.

Read: John 4:27-30

Listen: What is God saying to you through his word today? Write about it in your journal.

Reflect: Ultimately, God is a lover, in relentless pursuit of his beloved, just ask the woman at the well. She never would have come looking for him, so he had to go looking for her. The entire encounter is one he initiated. Why? To pursue her and then to awaken her to his passionate, relentless love. It was the only thing that could fill her thirsty soul. His love was the "living water" he kept telling her about. It's what she had been desperately looking for and searching for all of her life.

Once she finally recognized that fact, it happened — she was full. Look no further than the empty water jar she flung aside; she no longer needed it. She was finally full. She had finally found her beloved and wanted everyone to know it.

Respond: What water jar(s) do you need to leave behind? Will you?

Pray: Ask God to show you what water jars you still need to leave behind. Ask him to fill you to overflowing with his life and joy and love.

Lord Jesus, help us to overflow so abundantly with your life and your love that we pour forth your living water to anyone and everyone who crosses our paths. That's how ministry is designed to happen.

Rest: Rest in the presence of the One who sees you, knows you, and loves you.

February 4

Silence: "The Lord is in his holy temple; let all the earth be silent before him." (Habakkuk 2:20)

Opening Prayer: Lord Jesus, thank you that there is always more to you than meets the eye, more to you than we can fully know. Help us to see you more and more fully, so that we can worship you more and more rightly. Amen.

Read: Revelation 1:12-18

Listen: What is God saying to you through his word today? Write about it in your journal.

Reflect: Just when we think we have our picture of Jesus pretty concrete and familiar and well-defined, he comes along and blows the tiny little box we had him in to smithereens. This is no tame, serene, gentle Jesus, but a Jesus who is big and wild and glorious and awesome and free…and, to be honest, a little bit scary. So much so that the apostle John, who referred to himself as "the disciple whom Jesus loved," the same disciple who laid his head on Jesus' chest at the Last Supper, fell on his face in fearful reverence at the very sight of him. The Jesus in the book of Revelation is a Jesus we don't often *behold*. We would rather not, for that Jesus will not be reduced or tamed or managed or controlled.

But in order for us to know the real Jesus, and not just our westernized, watered-down version of him, this must be a part of our picture: eyes like blazing fire, feet like bronze glowing in a furnace, voice like the sound of rushing waters, and a sharp double-edged sword coming out of his mouth. Definitely a little different than the picture we are used to, but it's the same Jesus nonetheless.

If we truly want to know Jesus, we need to get to know all of him, not just the parts we are comfortable with. That's what's so great about the book of Revelation, it helps us to see Jesus in a whole new way.

Respond: How is this picture of Jesus different from the way you normally picture him? What does this picture of him stir up within you? How does it disturb or disrupt you? How does it comfort you? How does it challenge you?

Pray: Meditate for several minutes on the picture of Jesus from Revelation 1:12-16. What are you most drawn to about him? Why? Thank him for that.

Lord Jesus, help us to see you as you really are, so that we might worship you as you really deserve.

Rest: Rest in the presence of the One who sees you, knows you, and loves you.

February 5

Silence: "Guard your steps when you go to the house of God. Go near to listen rather than to offer the sacrifice of fools, who do not know they do wrong. Do not be quick with your mouth or hasty in your heart to utter anything before God. God is in heaven and you are on earth, so let your words be few." (Ecclesiastes 5:1-2)

Opening Prayer: Lord Jesus, help us to never, ever forsake you, our first and truest love.

Read: Revelation 2:1-7

Listen: What is God saying to you through his word today? Write about it in your journal.

Reflect: It is amazing how easily love can turn into duty, if we are not careful to keep the fires of romance alive deep in our hearts. Not that duty is a bad thing, mind you, but if that's all we've got, it is far from the passionate love that our hearts most deeply long for — particularly in relationship with God.

I wonder if that's what happened to the church at Ephesus? I wonder if, over time, their relationship with God turned from loving romance to routine duty. I wonder where, when, and why they just started going through the motions, rather than allowing themselves to be seized by the power of the Great Affection. Don't get me wrong, duty is a significant part of the commitment of love, but if our affections are not engaged as well, it will quickly digress into something not resembling love at all.

That seems to be what Jesus was getting at when he wrote the letter to the church at Ephesus. He not only wanted their actions, but also their affections. He wanted their hearts, not merely their behavior. For he knew that if he had their hearts, their behavior would follow.

He wanted the attention and affection and passion and intensity that there had been "at first." He wanted them to return to the days when all they could do was think about him and long for him and yearn to be with him in an intimate embrace of Divine Love.

So he called them to repent — which does not seem like a particularly romantic word, but is — and return to the Lover of their souls, who continually longs for intimate union with his beloved.

Respond: If Jesus wrote you a letter today, what would it say? Who or what is your first love these days? Who or what is Jesus' biggest competition for your affection?

Pray: Ask God to show you what your first love really is? Listen for his response.

Lord Jesus, always be my first and truest love.

Rest: Rest in the presence of the One who sees you, knows you, and loves you.

February 6

Silence: Be still and quiet for a few minutes. Allow the Spirit of God to prepare your heart and make space in your soul for him to speak.

Opening Prayer: Forgive us, Lord Jesus, when life becomes more about our own comfort and convenience and agenda, than about following you. For following you will always cost us our lives.

Read: Revelation 2:8-11

Listen: What is God saying to you through his word today? Write about it in your journal.

Reflect: The cost of following Jesus is high. It is easy to lose sight of that fact in the country we live in. For those of us in America, following Jesus has cost us very little, especially compared to those who live in other parts of the world. It seems that our culture is much like the one of the church in Laodicea, rather than Smyrna. That is probably why we can tend to be a little on the lazy and lukewarm side in our journey of faith; we have gotten far too comfortable.

So it is a little hard for us to imagine what it would be like to get a letter from God telling us, "*Do not fear what you are about to suffer.*" That would get our attention, wouldn't it? How would you deal with that kind of news? What would it do within you? Would it cause you immediate distress, or resolve? Would it make you determined to stand firm in the midst of the coming trial, or try to figure out how to escape or avoid it in any way you could? Would it cause your faith and trust in Jesus to be strengthened, or would it cause you to question the goodness of his heart? What if following Jesus was to cost you everything? It does, you know. What is your reaction to that?

You have to wonder how the church in Smyrna received this hard and challenging word, as well as the call that followed, *"Be faithful unto death and I will give you the crown of life."* I'd like to believe that they handled it with all of the courage and resolve that God hoped they would, realizing that this world was not their home, but only a temporary stop on the road to eternity. Realizing that life was not about them, but about God's Kingdom and his glory. Resolving that no cost was too great because of their immense love for their Lord and Savior, Jesus.

What about us? How have we somehow escaped the notion that following Jesus costs us everything? What has following Jesus cost you lately? How have you responded to that? Are you willing to give everything to him the way the church in Smyrna was being called to?

Respond: How would you respond if Jesus sent this letter to you? What would scare you? What would excite you? What does this letter tell you about Jesus?

Pray: Count the cost of following Jesus. What has following him cost you in your life thus far? Ask him what it's going to cost you in the future. Tell him how you feel about that. Tell him whether or not you are willing to truly follow him.

I will follow you, Lord Jesus, whatever the cost. Give me the courage and the strength and the grace to do so.

Rest: Rest in the presence of the One who sees you, knows you, and loves you.

February 7

Silence: Start today with silence; always start with silence. Your silence will allow you to hear God speak.

Opening Prayer: It is your voice, Lord Jesus, that sets us free. Because it is your voice, and not the voice of the world around us, that is right and true. Help us to listen to you, Lord Jesus, and not to the world. Amen.

Read: Revelation 2:12-17

Listen: What is God saying to you through his word today? Write about it in your journal.

Reflect: One of the constant struggles in the life of faith is to pay attention to the right voices and ignore the wrong ones. That would be especially true if you lived in a place like Pergamum. It was the heart of enemy territory; the capital city of evil. It was a place of indulgence, immorality, and deception. It was a place where the wrong voices abounded. And one of the chief strategies of the enemy is to try and make us believe things about ourselves and about our God that simply aren't true.

In an environment such as this, it is vital to hold fast to the truth lest we get sucked into one of these deceptive ways of thinking. For the truth is our greatest defense against the deceptions of the enemy. In fact, John tells us in one of his earlier writings that when we come to *know the truth, the truth will set us free* (John 8:32). Maybe that's why Jesus uses the image of a sword (his word) as the means by which he will wage war against the enemy. His truth is our main offensive weapon. It is the thing we can use to destroy the lies of the deceiver and hold fast to the truth of our creator. When we hold fast to the truth about our God and about ourselves we will be free men and women.

The truth is that our God is so filled with love for us that he has a special name picked out for each one of us—a pet name, if you will. It is a name of deep affection that will bear our true identity. One that will immediately let us know how incredibly valuable we are to him and how extravagantly loved we are by him. It is a name written on a white stone that he will share with us when we are united with him in the heavenly realms for all eternity. It is a name that is the truest expression of who we really are. It is a name that is just too good to be true, yet it is both too good and too true. And I am convinced that when we hear it, a deep "yes" will rise up from the core of our being. I can't wait.

Respond: Who does this world tell you that you are? What do the voices within you tell you? What names have you been called—by others or by yourself—that are hurtful and untrue? What effect have those names had on your life? What name do you think Jesus calls you by? How does that name change the way you live?

Pray: Ask Jesus to show you the painful name(s) that you have believed to be true about yourself. Now ask him to tell you what he calls you.

Lord Jesus, thank you that you have a name for me that is true, and more beautiful than I could ever imagine. It is a name of delight and affection. It is the name I want to live by every second of my life. Thank you that your name for me holds the truth of who I really am.

Rest: Rest in the presence of the One who sees you, knows you, and loves you.

February 8

Silence: "Be still and know that I am God." (Ps. 46:10) No, really. Right now. "Be still and know that I am God."

Opening Prayer: Lord Jesus, thank you that we are defined by your love, not by our own achievements and accomplishments, or even by our failures and mistakes. Please remind us of that each day. Then we will never feel the need to earn or prove anything, but will be free to love and free to be loved. Amen.

Read: Revelation 2:18-29

Listen: What is God saying to you through his word today? Write about it in your journal.

Reflect: Being tolerant is generally thought of as a positive virtue in this day and age. And in terms of being loving, caring, and accepting of those around us, that would seem to be a good and right thing. After all, didn't Jesus eat with *tax gatherers and sinners*? Wasn't it Jesus who said, "It is not the healthy who need a doctor, but the sick? For I have not come to call the righteous, but sinners." (Matthew 9:12-13) Jesus seemed at home with, and embracing of, people from all walks of life — people who were lost in an abundance of ways. So, we too, as his people, should always have a loving openness to people in this broken and hurting world.

But here in the letter to the church at Thyatira there is a different kind of tolerance that Jesus gives a pretty strong warning against. It seems that the people of this church were subtly being seduced into thinking that certain practices were okay, when the truth was that those very practices — ones they thought would have little to no impact on them individually or corporately — would actually impact them significantly… over time.

Thus, the message of Jesus to the church at Thyatira seems pretty simple, *"Watch what you tolerate, because, in the end, it can lead you miles away from your desired destination."* Oh it might not seem like a big deal at first. In fact, it could be a very subtle thing — only one or two degrees different from the intended course. The problem is that one or two degrees, over time, amounts to a pretty significant difference in the long run. In fact, it is an easy way to get lost. And Jesus doesn't want us lost, he wants us home. Therefore, he warns the church — not just the one at Thyatira, but of every time and every place — what an enormous impact tolerating a few things can have on our lives.

Respond: How would you respond if Jesus sent this letter to you? What would scare you? What would excite you? What does this letter tell you about Jesus? Where and how do you need to heed Jesus' warning about the things you tolerate? How does he want you to respond?

Pray: Ask Jesus to show you where you are tolerating things that are actually drawing you away from him. Listen for his response.

"Search me, O God, and know my heart; test me and know my anxious thoughts. See if there is any offensive way in me, and lead me in the way everlasting." (Psalm 139:23-24)

Rest: Rest in the presence of the One who sees you, knows you, and loves you.

February 9

Silence: Stop. Sit. Be still. Be quiet. Pay attention. Listen. That's how we make room for God.

Opening Prayer: Lord Jesus, help us to never be concerned with merely keeping up appearances. You care about what's really going on within us, not just what people think is going on. Help us to be true and real and genuine and sincere—just like you.

Read: Revelation 3:1-6

Listen: What is God saying to you through his word today? Write about it in your journal.

Reflect: A reputation is a powerful thing. Because a reputation (good or bad) is often not reality, but only someone's impression of reality. And in our day and age—as well as that of the church at Sardis apparently—impression is everything. If you can create and maintain the impression you are hoping for, then who cares what the reality is, right? Thus, reputation becomes all about impression management. What people think about you becomes more important to you than what the truth about you really is. As long as you can keep up the charade, it's all good. But keeping up the charade can be exhausting, and darn near impossible over time. Eventually someone is going to find out the ugly truth. There is always that one person in any crowd who is adept at spotting a phony. Someone who is either magically or supernaturally able to see right through the façade—right down to the core. And when this happens we are horrified. Because somehow our greatest fear—and maybe in a strange way our deepest longing—comes true: we are exposed.

That's how the church at Sardis must've felt. They had worked and worked at maintaining a good reputation, even though they knew deep in their hearts that there was no life in them. And then, along came Jesus, entering into the midst of the pretense, calling their bluff, tearing their finely crafted costumes to smithereens, and putting them in scramble mode.

What could they do? Deny it? Ignore it? Avoid it? Rationalize? Or would they resort to attack? What is the best strategy for damage control? How could they spin it so that their reputation, which they worked so hard on, would still come out intact?

But maybe there was another solution. Maybe the answer was to do exactly what Jesus was suggesting—admit the truth. Maybe it was time to come clean and stop trying to fool everyone. Maybe they should take Jesus' words as a wake-up call and start living authentically, with God and with others. Maybe it was time to repent, to change their way of thinking, as well as their way of living, and begin to see everything, and live everything, differently.

Maybe they needed to realize that reality was more important than reputation, and start trying to be authentic people in Christ. People more concerned with how they were loving than with what people were thinking. Maybe they needed to start being more like Jesus, who *"made himself of no reputation, and took upon him the form of a servant, and was made in the likeness of men: and being found in fashion as a man, humbled himself, and became obedient unto death, even the death of the cross."* (Philippians 2:7-8, KJV)

A man can dream, right?

Respond: Where in your life are you just keeping up appearances? Where are you more worried about reputation than reality? How will you begin to live more authentically?

Pray: Ask God to show you the places in your life where you are more concerned with appearances than authenticity? Ask him to make you the truest version of yourself.

Lord Jesus, you know me better than I know myself. Show me where I am just pretending, and show me where I am being who I really am. Help me to be more concerned with being godly than with being popular.

Rest: Rest in the presence of the One who sees you, knows you, and loves you.

February 10

Silence: Seek the quiet around you and then listen to the Voice within you.

Opening Prayer: Lord Jesus, thank you that you are the God who opens doors. Show me the doors you have opened before me and give me the faith to step through them. Amen.

Read: Revelation 3:7-13

Listen: What is God saying to you through his word today? Write about it in your journal.

Reflect: Nothing is more inviting, and more terrifying, than an open door; especially a door that has been opened by God. And that is the image we have before us: God has set an open door before us, which no one is able to shut. What is this mysterious open door, and what is the invitation that it beckons us to? That is for each one of us to find out for ourselves.

The excitement of the open door comes from its limitless possibilities, and the terror is due to the fact that every open door requires us to take a step. Taking a step is an act of faith that flows from a heart of trust. And an open door is of no value at all if we do not step through it.

The Message translation of Romans 5:2 says it so well, when it states: *"We throw open our doors to God and discover at the same moment that he has already thrown open his door to us. We find ourselves standing where we always hoped we might stand – out in the wide open spaces of God's grace and glory, standing tall and shouting our praise."*

What door has God opened for you these days? Will you have the courage to step through it? If not, you will never get to see the beauty and the wonder that's waiting on the other side.

Respond: How would you respond if Jesus sent this letter to you? What would scare you about it? What would excite you? What does this letter tell you about Jesus? What doors is Jesus opening around or within you these days? What is his invitation to you? Will you step through it?

Pray: Ask Jesus to show you the doors he is opening, both for you and in you. Ask him for the wisdom to see them and the courage to step through them.

O Jesus, give me the wisdom to see the doors you are opening in and around me, and give me the courage and the strength and the grace to step through them.

Rest: Rest in the presence of the One who sees you, knows you, and loves you.

February 11

Silence: Silence is not a luxury, but a necessity. And, most often, the reason we don't have any silence is because we choose not to. When we are finally willing to acknowledge its importance, and make it a priority, it will happen. It is not something we find time for, but something we make time for.

Opening Prayer: Lord Jesus, forgive me when my heart doesn't burn with zealous love for you. The truth is that I don't like lukewarm-ness any more than you do. So stoke the fires of love deep within me, so that I might be consumed with love and desire for you. Amen.

Read: Revelation 3:14-22

Listen: What is God saying to you through his word today? Write about it in your journal.

Reflect: The church at Laodicea was tepid. Wealth and prosperity had lulled them to sleep spiritually. Or, to use the term John uses here, they had become lukewarm. And lukewarm-ness is a trait that God doesn't care for at all. Come to think of it, nobody cares for it. Because being lukewarm reeks of apathy. It has no backbone to it, no commitment, no passion, no zeal. Which is one of the things God asks the church at Laodicea to become—*zealous*. The word zealous in the Greek is *zēloō*, which means "to boil." God longs for their hearts to boil with love for him. In other words, God is telling them to *turn up the heat* of their affection for him and be lukewarm no longer.

The image of a stove immediately comes to mind. God is saying, "Right now your passion for me is about a four or five (out of ten). Is that good enough for you? Because it is not good enough for me. I didn't create you to be just a four or five, so *turn up the heat*. I want more for you and I want more from you. Don't settle for less."

I think that's why I love this passage; it is an invitation. God is inviting us into a deeper, more intimate, more passionate relationship with him. God wants our inner lives to boil with affection and desire for him.

The reality is that we all boil inside for something. There is something in our lives that is getting our passion, something that is on our "front burner." It might be work, it might be family, it might be a significant relationship, it might be wealth, or it might even be ministry. Something is on the front burner of our lives, receiving the heat of our affections—a place that only God deserves. Our challenge is to take the time and the space to figure out what the main object of our affections really is, to name it, and to repent—to return God to his rightful place on the front burner of our lives.

One of the ways we do that is given right in the text—by simply opening the door to him, the One who *stands at the door and knocks.* We must consistently open the door of our hearts and invite him in, so that we can spend intimate time with him at the table of our souls, feasting on the Bread of Life. He will not intrude. He will wait until space has been made, the door has been opened, and he has been welcomed in. May we all hear the knock and open the door each day to make space and time for him.

Respond: How would you feel if Jesus sent this letter to you? What does this letter show you about him? What word would you use to describe the state of your spiritual life? Why? What is on the *front burner* of your life? What would it look like to turn the *heat up* on your life with God? What would it take to move him to the front burner of your heart?

Pray: Ask God to show you what is on the front burner of your life? Ask him to help you put Jesus there.

Lord Jesus, you want all of my attention and all of my affection. Help me to love you enough to give you both.

Rest: Rest in the presence of the One who sees you, knows you, and loves you.

February 12

Silence: "Come to me, all you who are weary and burdened, and I will give you rest." (Mt. 11:28) Let your soul become still and quiet in the presence of Jesus today.

Opening Prayer: I lift my eyes to the hills, where does my help come from? My help comes from the Lord, the maker of heaven and earth. (Psalm 121:1-2)

Read: Hebrews 12:1-2

Listen: What is God saying to you through his word today? Write about it in your journal.

Reflect: In the spiritual life, where we fix our eyes is everything. If we allow our eyes to be consumed by our own struggles, our own surroundings, and our own circumstances, our hearts will be full of the worry, anxiety, and strife. But if we are able to fix our eyes on the bigger picture, and not on whatever troubles we may be experiencing at the moment — if we are able to take out eyes off of ourselves and fix them on Jesus — everything changes. Oh, the circumstances themselves may not change much, but the spirit we have in the midst of those circumstances, and our quality of life as a result, will change immensely.

I guess that's why the Scriptures talk so much about it: *I lift my eyes to you, to you whose throne is in heaven.* (Ps. 123:1) *So we fix our eyes not on what is see, but on what is unseen. For what is seen is temporary, but what is unseen is eternal.* (2 Cor. 4:18) *Let us fix our eyes on Jesus, the author and perfecter of our faith, who for the joy set before him endured the cross, scorning its shame, and sat down at the right hand of the throne of God.* (Heb. 12:2)

It is really not all that complicated — in theory at least — but it is a little more difficult in practice. When our eyes are consumed with ourselves, we find ourselves filled with insecurity, anxiety, and fear. It's a downward spiral that is incredibly difficult to break free from, which can cause us to get stuck inside ourselves. But when we are able to fix our eyes on Jesus instead, something beautiful happens. Somehow he gives us the ability to climb out of the dark pit of self and come into the light of love.

It is an invitation that is always open to us. *"Look at me,"* says our Savior, *"and you will be able to experience the joy and the life and the peace that I desire for you, rather than trying so hard to provide it for yourself."*

Respond: What are your eyes focused on these days? What impact is it having on you? How might you fix your eyes of Jesus instead?

Pray: Ask God to show you where your eyes are focused these days. Ask him for the grace and the discipline to fix your eyes on Jesus.

O God, sometimes I get stuck inside myself, consumed with my own little life. When I do this, my life is filled with insecurity, anxiety, and fear. You want so much more for me than that, so help me to fix my eyes on you, Lord Jesus. Let your love conquer my insecurity, let your peace replace my anxiety, and let my trust in you overcome my fear. I pray this by your power and in your name. Amen.

Rest: Rest in the presence of the One who sees you, knows you, and loves you.

February 13

Silence: Sit quietly in the presence of your Heavenly Father today. Enjoy his presence. Enjoy him enjoying you.

Opening Prayer: O God, more than anything else you want us to know you as our Father. Not a distant, disinterested, stern, or angry father, but the Father we always dreamt about in our wildest dreams. A Father that is loving and strong, tender and true, present and attentive. That is the kind of Father you are, and we are so grateful to be your children.

Read: Matthew 6:5-13

Listen: What is God saying to you through his word today? Write about it in your journal.

Reflect: *"Our Father in heaven."* The guiding image for our prayers, Jesus tells us, is that of God as "Our Father." It is an image of strong, tender, and unfailing love. Thus, our Father-God has a special affection for the sound of our voice; it brings him deep joy and gladness. He longs for us to be near to him so he can breathe in our scent, delight over our features, run his hands through our hair, and press his lips to our cheeks. It seems like that alone would be enough reason for us to want to pray.

Respond: What does the image of God as your Father stir up in you today? How does it affect the way you pray? How could it?

Pray: Sit and enjoy your Father-God for a few minutes today, and let him enjoy you.

Our Father in heaven. Thank you that that's who you are!

Rest: Rest in the presence of the One who sees you, knows you, and loves you.

February 14

Silence: So many things clutter our hearts and minds. If we do not take time to be still and quiet, they will dominate our inner space and leave us no room to really hear from God, much less behold him. Spend a few minutes in stillness and silence today before we begin. Get in touch with yourself, and with your God.

Opening Prayer: Lord Jesus, you are the only one who really sees me, really knows me, and really loves me. Help me to know that I have no hope of really seeing others, until I have been seen by you. Otherwise, I will spend all my time and energy trying way too hard to be seen by them.

Read: Luke 7:36-50

Listen: What is God saying to you through his word today? Write about it in your journal.

Reflect: *Then he turned toward the woman and said to Simon, "Do you see this woman?" (Luke 7:44)*

Okay, I get it. Seeing is always a two way street. How we see things is always determined by our own inner dynamics at the time. In order to be able to see people (and things) the way they really are, we must first be truly seen by the One who made us, the One who knows us, and the One who loves us. Without first being seen, known, and loved by Him, we will always be far too consumed and concerned with the way we are being seen by others. We will live in order to prove our own worthiness, rather than living because the One who made us has pronounced us worthy. We will live in order to achieve an identity, rather than living because He has already bestowed an identity upon us.

That was certainly the case with Simon the Pharisee. He was so consumed with himself that he was unable to see what was right in front of him. He was so full of his own insecurities and fears that he had no room to see the beauty of what had just taken place between Jesus and this *sinful woman*. He was so busy criticizing and comparing and trying to convince himself and his world that he was worthy of love, that he was unable to see the passion and the affection and the beauty of her gesture. Because when you are consumed with yourself, you can never see others for who and what they really are; they become threats and competitors rather than fellow pilgrims and travelers.

Simon could see nothing but himself, so Jesus had to take a moment to help him see the situation for what it really was. He pointed out the beauty of the woman's act of love, as well as Simon's lack thereof. In helping Simon *see* the woman, Jesus had also helped Simon *see* himself. For only after we have been seen, do we have any hope of seeing others the way God intended for us to.

Respond: How well are you really seeing others these days? How is that related to how aware you are of being seen by Jesus? How will you increase your awareness of both?

Pray: Ask God to help you see him, yourself, and others today.

Thank you that you see me, Lord Jesus, wherever I am, whatever I am doing, and whatever is going on in my life. And because of that I have the freedom to see, know, and love others. Thanks be to God! Amen.

Rest: Rest in the presence of the One who sees you, knows you, and loves you.

February 15

Silence: Be still my soul, the Lord is on thy side. Bear patiently the cross of grief or pain. Leave to thy God to order and provide. In every age he faithful will remain. Be still my soul: thy best, thy heavenly friend, through thorny ways leads to a joyful end.

Opening Prayer: You are the God who sees me. I have now seen the One who sees me. (Gen. 16:13, NIV)

Read: Genesis 16:1-16

Listen: What is God saying to you through his word today? Write about it in your journal.

Reflect: "I have now seen the One who sees me." Is that not a great phrase? There is something really beautiful about being seen, but there is something even more beautiful about seeing the One who sees you.

A few years ago, in the middle of the summer, I was at our local high school watching our football team as they were in the midst of summer workouts. I had been the chaplain of the team for about 15 years at that point and, to be quite honest, on that particular day I was really discouraged. I wondered if it was all worth it—all the time, all the energy, all the investment. I wondered if I was making any difference at all. In short, I was feeling really unseen—invisible, in fact.

Anyway, the team was on the field with the backs and receivers on one end and the linemen on the other. All of the sudden one of our receivers looked down to where the linemen were working and called out to one of his teammates, "I see you! I see you, Michael! I see you, 5-8!"

And I instantly realized that the voice I had just heard was for me. It was God, reminding me that he sees me, and that was all that really mattered. I had seen the One who sees me, and it changed everything.

God sees you too, you know—wherever you are, whatever is going on in your life, whatever the state of your heart. Whatever your level of loneliness or desperation or pain, he sees you. And he wants you to know that. You are not alone. This very day he wants you to see the One who sees you, because when that happens it changes everything. Just ask Hagar.

Respond: Where have you come from and where are you going? How does it make you feel to know that God cares enough to ask you those questions? How can you relate to Hagar these days? How do you long to be seen by God today? What does it do within you to see the One who sees you?

Pray: Be seen by the God who sees you in prayer today.

O God, thank you that you see me. Help me to see you, the One who sees me. And then help me to see others with those very same eyes. Amen.

Rest: Rest in the presence of the One who sees you, knows you, and loves you.

February 16

Silence: "I have stilled and quieted my soul, like a weaned child with its mother; like a weaned child is my soul within me." (Psalm 131:2)

Opening Prayer: Lord Jesus, thank you that you see me. You see the deepest longings of my heart and you want me to know what those are, as well as where they came from. Thank you that you care enough to ask me the question, "What are you seeking?"

Read: John 1:35-42

Listen: What is God saying to you through his word today? Write about it in your journal.

Reflect: What Jesus *saw* when he turned around was a group of curious seekers. A couple of men who had heard something that made them long for more than the life they were currently living. Some fishermen who, for some reason, unknown even to themselves, had been lured out into the desert by the voice of one who spoke with power and authority.

That is what Jesus *saw* when he looked into their hearts. He saw a longing. He saw a deep yearning. And he realized that these men needed to *see* it too. So he asked them what would prompt such odd behavior: "*What are you seeking?* What do you want? Why in the world did you come all the way out here? What were you hoping to find?" And when he asked the question, they knew immediately that they had been *seen*.

What about you? How would you answer that question today? What are you seeking? He sees you, you know. He sees the deepest longings and yearnings of your heart. Otherwise, he wouldn't have asked.

Respond: What are you seeking? How does it make you feel to know that God knows the answer to that question and wants you to know it as well?

Pray: Ask Jesus to show you what you are seeking, and listen for his reply.

Lord Jesus, show me what I'm really seeking. For regardless of what I tell myself, ultimately, I am seeking you.

Rest: Rest in the presence of the One who sees you, knows you, and loves you.

February 17

Silence: Calm the voices that resound within you and allow your heart and your soul to become still and quiet. This will make it possible for you to hear the voice of God, however and whenever he cares to speak.

Opening Prayer: Your eyes, Lord Jesus, see into the very depths of my soul, which both thrills me and terrifies me. Yet when you look at me, you always look through the eyes of love. Help me to know what is the most true and beautiful about me, and help me to live out of that place of truth and beauty. For only then will I be the person you made me to be — the very best version of myself. Amen.

Read: John 1:43-51

Listen: What is God saying to you through his word today? Write about it in your journal.

Reflect: When Jesus sees Nathanael, he really sees him. In fact, he sees right into him; nothing is hidden. And when he sees deeply into the heart and soul of this man, what does he bring attention to? He brings attention to what is true and beautiful. He sees a man being exactly who and what God intended him to be, nothing false—no hiding, no masking, no posturing, no proving. How beautiful is that?

And you can tell by Nathanael's response that he had truly been seen. "How do you know me?" he replied. He didn't disagree with Jesus, because Jesus had spoken to his deepest parts. Jesus had recognized what was most true and spoken into that. Not to say that Nathanael was perfect, obviously he wasn't. But what Jesus saw, and chose to call attention to, was the fact that deep within Nathanael was a longing to live truly. He saw a man attempting to be the best, God-breathed version of himself.

I love this story because I live with the desire to be seen as well. Not just the screwed up, messy, insecure, neurotic parts of myself—my worst self, that is—but the good and true and beautiful parts of myself. I long for those parts to be seen and acknowledged and called forth, so that I am drawn to live more and more out of my best, God-intended self each minute of each day. I love that this seems to be Jesus' desire as well.

And not only is it his desire for me, but it is his desire for how I go about seeing and relating to others. In essence, it is what true ministry is all about—really seeing people, really knowing people, and really loving people. People are dying to be seen, known, and loved, and if we follow Jesus' example here that's just what we will do. We will go about our days with our eyes wide open, looking beyond the surface of things and of people, and seeing into their depths. Once we do that, we can begin to draw out and call forth that which is most true and beautiful about them.

Respond: What does Jesus see when he looks into you today? What is most true? What is most beautiful? What does he long to touch and transform?

Pray: Ask Jesus what he sees in you, and listen for his reply.

See me today, Lord Jesus, and help me to see myself as you see me, so that I may begin to see others that way as well.

Rest: Rest in the presence of the One who sees you, knows you, and loves you.

February 18

Silence: If we ever hope to be able to hear God's voice or to see his face, silence and solitude are likely to be a significant part of the equation. Spend a few minutes in silence today as a way of preparing the soil of your soul to receive whatever he might have for you.

Opening Prayer: Lord Jesus, when I see you I see the One who sees me all the way to the core: part of which I love and part of which I hate. For you see things in me that I do not particularly want you to see, things I do not even want to see myself. You see all the ways I do not really want to *get well*. You see my real fears and my real motives and my real insecurities, and you long for me to rise above all of those. Give me the strength and the courage to leave behind my dysfunctional ways of being and seeing, and come and follow you. Amen.

Read: John 5:1-15

Listen: What is God saying to you through his word today? Write about it in your journal.

Reflect: God sees our pain. God sees our struggle. God sees our hopelessness and despair. God even sees our weariness and exhaustion. After all, he is *the God who sees*. Jesus shows us that.

But what was it about this particular man that caught the eye of Jesus that day? After all, there were multitudes of sick people laying around the pool. Why did Jesus focus on him?

Was it how long he had been there? Was it how often he had tried to get into the pool? Was it because there was *no one there to help him*? Who knows? But for some reason he got the attention of the Savior.

"Do you want to get well?" The question is as simple as it is profound, especially for someone who may have gotten used to a certain pattern of existence over the last thirty-eight years. Healing can be disruptive. Old patterns die hard, which is exactly why the question is so insightful. Maybe he had gotten so used to this way of life that being healed would turn his whole world upside down.

Seeing the God who sees you is not always a comfortable thing; it can be very unsettling. Maybe life on the mat had gotten oddly comfortable and safely familiar, so much so that he was willing to settle for less than the life Jesus wanted for him. We do it all the time. When we come face-to-face with Jesus it means that we have to leave our old ways and patterns and dysfunctions behind, and it can be terrifying.

But the beautiful thing is that Jesus didn't allow the man to stay where he was, and he doesn't allow us that luxury either. He calls each of us, just like he did the man by the pool, to "Get up! Pick up your mat and walk."

Will you? Do you want to get well? Do you really?

Respond: Do you want to get well? Really? What will that mean for you? What *mat* do you need to leave behind? Will you *get up*?

Pray: Listen to Jesus as he asks you, "Do you want to get well?" Give him your answer. What does that mean in your life? Now, hear him say the words, "Get up. Pick up your mat and walk." Will you?

I do want to get well, Lord Jesus, but I am so scared. I have grown so comfortable in my dysfunction that getting well is liable to turn my life upside down. Give me the strength and the courage and the grace to *get up* and leave my *mat* behind. I want to experience the life and the love and the wholeness you created me for. Please do not let me settle for *life on the mat* any longer. Have mercy on me, Lord Jesus.

Rest: Rest in the presence of the One who sees you, knows you, and loves you.

February 19

Silence: If you will just be still and listen, I will come to you. I will speak and I will move and I will stir and I will draw near. All you have to do is be still.

Opening Prayer: O God, you love us with a Father's heart — waiting, watching, yearning, and hoping for our return home. And then running out to meet us as we finally come back to you. That is not merely a one-time thing, but an everyday thing. So help us to return to you once again today.

Read: Luke 15:20-24

Listen: What is God saying to you through his word today? Write about it in your journal.

Reflect: The eyes of love have been on the front porch day after day, night after night, watching and waiting and hoping. Through the autumn rains and the winter snows, through the spring flowers and the summer's heat, they have not stopped searching the countryside for the sight of the one who had left home in pursuit of a life and a love that could not possibly match the one he had left behind.

The heart of a father is such a beautiful thing, filled with love and affection for those who are his, regardless of what they do or where they wander. And the heart of this Father is the most beautiful of all. He had loved his son enough to let him go and now all he could do was wait and hope that that very same love would one day draw his beloved son back home again.

Well, that *one day* finally came. Way out on the horizon he saw a movement. "Could it be?" he thought. His heart began to pound. "Could this finally be the day?" He stood up from his chair and stepped to the porch rail to get a better look. His heart leaped within him. There he was; it was really him. Still *a long way off*, but definitely him.

It was one of the most beautiful sights he had seen in his entire life. The eyes of love are always 20/20; they always see the right things. These eyes did not pay attention to the dirt and the grime. They did not care about the slop in his hair or the dung on his shoes. They did not see a disappointment or a failure or a rebel, they only saw a son—a son who was fully and deeply and unconditionally loved.

At the sight of this son returning home the Father could not contain himself. He threw caution (and dignity) to the wind and began running through the fields to meet him. After all, his son *was lost* and had now been *found*. For unlike some other fathers, the eyes of this Father were (and still are) full of love, not judgment. First he ran, then he embraced, then he kissed, and then he celebrated this one who had been gone, but who had now come home again.

And he still does that today. It's just who he is. So come on home, son or daughter, whatever that may mean. Come on home. The Father's eyes are full of love for you and he can't wait to have you back in his loving arms again.

Respond: How do you really think God sees you? How does that play itself out in your life? What would happen if you really believed the Father looks at you through the eyes of love?

Pray: Ask God to show you how he sees you. Look into his eyes and see the depths of his love and affection. Allow his love to capture you, to consume you, and to transform you.

Lord Jesus, help me to really believe it's true. You love me beyond my wildest dreams.

Rest: Rest in the presence of the One who sees you, knows you, and loves you.

February 20

Silence: We have been given the work of slowing and quieting and uncrowding ours hearts, so that there will be space within us to see God's hand, to sense his stirring, and to hear his voice. If we truly want to *behold* Jesus, it will not happen without silence and stillness.

Opening Prayer: Lord Jesus, thank you that you look at me and love me. Show me how fully, deeply, and unconditionally I am loved today, and let it change everything about me.

Read: Mark 10:17-23

Listen: What is God saying to you through his word today? Write about it in your journal.

Reflect: He had it all, or so it seemed—wealth, power, and youth. Who could ask for anything more? And yet something was still missing, otherwise he would never have come to Jesus with his question: "What do I still lack?" (Mt. 19:20) And what a gutsy question it was; a question coming from a truly seeking heart. And a question that stirred the heart of the Savior. Just look his the response: *"Jesus looked at him and loved him."* As if to say, "I love that you are asking the question. Not many people come to me with such courage and honesty."

And the answer Jesus gave him was given out of that same love: "One thing you lack. Go, sell everything you have and give to the poor, and you will have treasure in heaven. Then come, follow me."

It was not an attempt to shame, or belittle, or put him in his place; it was an honest answer to an honest question. Jesus *saw* deeper than just his outward appearance; Jesus *saw* his heart and he loved what he saw. "If you really want to have eternal life, it will not come from your power, your youth, or your many possessions. It will only come from making me your treasure. Go, sell everything else, give it to those who really need it, and come follow me." It was a beautiful, if not incredibly demanding, invitation.

We do not know exactly why the young man *walked away sad*. Maybe he was unwilling to pay such a great price. Or, on the other hand, maybe he was. All we do know is that the eyes of love looked right into his heart and answered his deepest question: "What do I still lack?"

Are we willing to look into the eyes of love today and ask the same question? Are we willing to come to Jesus with our deepest longings and trust that he will give us the only answer that will truly satisfy our hearts and souls? And then are we willing to really trust his answer?

Respond: What does this story tell you about Jesus? What does it tell you about yourself? What do you *still lack*? Is Jesus your *one thing*? How does it make you feel to know that he looks at you and loves you?

Pray: Ask Jesus to show you what the most important thing in your life is. Wait for his response.

Lord Jesus, I don't ever want you to become the *one thing I still lack*, so help me to put you first in my life each and every day.

Rest: Rest in the presence of the One who sees you, knows you, and loves you.

February 21

Silence: Believe it or not, silence is necessary for our spiritual health the same way inhaling is essential for our physical health. We cannot live our lives in a constant exhale; we must learn how to inhale as well. Therefore, stop and spend a few minutes in silence. Breathe God into your tired and weary soul. Let his breath give you life and health and peace.

Opening Prayer: Lord Jesus, help us to tell your beautiful truth with our lives before we ever try to tell it with our words. For until we embody the truth we proclaim, why would anyone want to listen to what we have to say in the first place?

Read: Matthew 7:1-6

Listen: What is God saying to you through his word today? Write about it in your journal.

Reflect: Telling the truth always begins with telling it to yourself. Until we have come face-to-face with our own sin and need and dysfunction, we can never properly enter into the sin and need and dysfunction of others. There is a deep humility required—a realization of our own extreme brokenness. That realization creates a right spirit as we enter into the pain and struggle of others.

Unfortunately, however, throughout the centuries truth has been used as more of a weapon than a help. But truth was never intended to bludgeon, it was meant to awaken. So telling the truth should be something that draws rather than repels. Or as Emily Dickinson so beautifully put it, "The Truth must dazzle gradually."

Therefore, we must first live the truth before we ever run off to tell the truth. The truth must dazzle with our lives before it can dazzle with our words. That's why people were so drawn to Jesus; he embodied the truth he proclaimed. He was not a living contradiction, and we should not be either.

Respond: What word of truth do you need to hear today? How does that word need to be made flesh in your life? How should that affect the way you share the truth with others?

Pray: Ask Jesus to tell you the truth about yourself today? What do you hear? Ask him how he wants that truth to shape you and set you free?

Dazzle us gradually, Lord Jesus, with your truth, for it is truly beautiful. And once we have been captured by that truth, give us the wisdom to know how to tell others about it, not only with our words, but with our lives. Amen.

Rest: Rest in the presence of the One who sees you, knows you, and loves you.

February 22

Silence: "For God alone my soul waits in silence." (Psalm 62:1) Wait in silence for God alone.

Opening Prayer: Lord Jesus, please help me to have the strength and the grace and the courage to do whatever you ask of me, even if it's something I don't have the ability to do on my own.

Read: Mark 3:1-5

Listen: What is God saying to you through his word today? Write about it in your journal.

Reflect: *"Stretch out your hand."* It is what you told the man in the synagogue, and it is what you are telling me. But what does that mean, Lord Jesus? What are you really asking of me?

Are you asking me to have the courage to be vulnerable and powerless and weak, so that your strength and power might be on full display? Are you asking me to trust in your goodness and mercy, even when it demands that I do something that is impossible unless you give me the ability? Are you asking me to have faith in you to transform the parts of my life that are twisted and distorted and not at all what you intended them to be? Or are you simply asking me to obey, whether I understand what you are doing to or not?

Whatever the case, Lord Jesus, today you ask me to, *"Stretch out your hand."* Give me the wisdom to know exactly what that means, and the strength and the courage and the grace necessary to do it.

Respond: What does "Stretch out your hand" mean for you? What is Jesus really asking of you? Will you do it?

Pray: Hear Jesus as he tells you to "Stretch out your hand." What is the tone in his voice? What is the look in his eyes? Ask him what he is really asking you to do and listen for his reply.

Open and obedient, that's what you ask of me, Lord Jesus. Help me to be both. Amen.

Rest: Rest in the presence of the One who sees you, knows you, and loves you.

February 23

Silence: Spend a few minutes allowing your heart to grow still and quiet before the Lord. Hopefully you are getting used to this by now and it is becoming easier. If not, no worries, just continue to gently and steadily turn your heart to him.

Opening Prayer: Thank you, O Lord, that you care enough to draw us into your great heart of love. What a gift! Give us the wisdom and the grace to receive that gift each day. Amen.

Read: John 6:44

Listen: What is God saying to you through his word today? Write about it in your journal.

Reflect: Why me, O Lord? Why did you choose to lay your hand of love upon my life? There are so many others who are so much more deserving, so many others more gifted, more talented, and more accomplished. So why did you set your affection on me and draw my wandering heart to you? Of all the people it could have been, why did you choose me?

And why do you continue to give me this amazing life with you? Why do you grace me with deep intimacy and union? Why do you continually draw your mouth close to my ear and whisper words of delight and affection? Why do you keep on blessing my life in so many ways?

Why would you even desire a relationship with me in the first place? Why would choose to live in my broken and wayward heart? Why would you choose to allow me to be a part of your life and your love and your ministry? Why would you allow me the joy and the privilege of sharing in your sufferings?

It is all so much more than I could ask or dream or imagine. Why me, O Lord, why me?

Respond: How did God first draw your heart to himself? How has God been drawing you lately? What is your response?

Pray: Ask God to show you all of the ways he is (and has been) drawing your heart to him.

It's you, O Lord, it's all you. You are the pursuer, the initiator, and the romancer. You are the God who draws hearts. Draw our hearts to yourself this day and every day.

Rest: Rest in the presence of the One who sees you, knows you, and loves you.

February 24

Silence: Ask God to still and quiet your soul today. Ask him for the grace to be attentive and receptive to him.

Opening Prayer: Forgive me, Lord Jesus, when I try to live out of strength, rather than out of weakness. Forgive me when I try to rely on myself, rather than on your grace. Forgive me for not believing that your grace is enough for me.

Read: 2 Corinthians 12:8-9

Listen: What is God saying to you through his word today? Write about it in your journal.

Reflect: "My grace is sufficient for you. It really is. Whatever you are going through, whatever burden you are carrying, whatever situation you are struggling with, whatever thing you cannot fix. Whatever uncertainty you are facing, whatever battle you are fighting, whatever challenge is before you. Whatever demon you can't conquer, whatever pattern you can't break, whatever hole you have dug for yourself, there is always hope because my grace is sufficient for you. I can take your weakness and your powerlessness, I can take your brokenness and your vulnerability, and I can display my power. Trust me." ~Jesus

Respond: Where in your life is Jesus saying, "My grace is sufficient for you"? Is it? Is his grace enough for you?

Pray: Ask God to pour out his grace upon you, and upon those to whom you have been given. Let his grace be enough.

Lord Jesus, forgive us for not believing that your grace alone is sufficient for us. Help us to genuinely believe that you are all we need.

Rest: Rest in the presence of the One who sees you, knows you, and loves you.

February 25

Silence: "He who has ears, let him hear." That is impossible to do if you are not still and quiet. So, be still and quiet before the

Lord for a few minutes. Shut your mouth and open you ears, so that you might be able to hear his voice.

Opening Prayer: Sing your song of love deeply and tenderly into my life today, O Lord. Draw me into your divine embrace, capture my heart, and seize me with the power of your great affection. Let my life always be an overflow of your divine life and love.

Read: Revelation 2:2-5

Listen: What is God saying to you through his word today? Write about it in your journal.

Reflection:

> you have substituted
> busyness for intimacy
>
> you have confused
> being busy for me
> with being in love
> with me
>
> and that makes me
> really sad

Respond: Who or what is your first love these days? What does your life say about that? What does the way you spend your time say? What would it look like to make Jesus your first love?

Pray: Ask Jesus to show you where busyness and hurry has robbed him of your time and attention. Listen for his reply.

Lord Jesus, may you always be my first love. May you always be my first and truest affection. Open my ears to hear your word and open my eyes to see your face. Give me a life that is in perfect union with you.

Rest: Rest in the presence of the One who sees you, knows you, and loves you.

February 26

Silence: If you came into the presence of royalty, what would you do? What would you say? What should you say? The right answer is "not a thing." You would come in silent reverence for the One into whose presence you were entering. Jesus is a friend, no doubt, but he is also a king. In fact, he is *the* King. Come before him in silent reverence today.

Opening Prayer: Thank you, Lord Jesus, that you are far bigger and much more glorious than our little minds can ever conceive or imagine. You are the Alpha and the Omega, the Beginning and the End, the Eternal God. You are the One who was and who is and who is to come.

Read: John 8:48-59

Listen: What is God saying to you through his word today? Write about it in your journal.

Reflect: "Who do you think you are?" Can you image asking the Son of God that question? And if you were Jesus, could you imagine giving an answer. What answer could they possibly understand?

So Jesus used the same name God used at the burning bush: I AM. "Before Abraham was, I AM." Or, as John Piper so beautifully said, "Jesus speaks from God, and for God and as God" all at the same time, by just stating his name.

It's kind of like Jesus was saying, "I AM bigger, more glorious, and more powerful than you could ever imagine. The tiny little boxes you try to put me in can't possibly hold me, because I AM so much more than you can ever know or understand. You can try to control me, but I AM uncontrollable. You can try to tame and domesticate me, but I AM wild and free. I will not be contrived, manipulated, or controlled. I AM the first and the last, the Alpha and the Omega, the beginning and the end, the Eternal God. I am the visible image of the invisible God. If you want to know what God is really like, just look at me.

I AM. It was a name Jesus would use in the Gospel of John to describe himself in a number of different ways, all of which were meant to give us a bigger and deeper and fuller picture of the One we can never get our minds around.

Respond: What does the name I AM mean to you? What does it tell you about Jesus? How does it expand your picture and understanding of him?

Pray: Spend a few minutes in prayer simply beholding the Great I AM. Worship and adore him. Bow down before him.

Words fail me, Lord Jesus. How can I possibly use mere words to tell you how great and mighty and wonderful you are? Continue to expand my vision of you each and every day, so that I might know you more deeply and love you more dearly.

Rest: Rest in the presence of the One who sees you, knows you, and loves you.

February 27

Silence: It's amazing what a little stillness and silence in our lives and in our hearts will make room for. Make room for God right now by becoming still and silent before him.

Opening Prayer: Lord Jesus, Bread of Life, be food for our hungry souls today, so that we might eat of you and be satisfied. Only then will we have anything to offer the hungry and broken in our world. We can only feed them, if you first feed us.

Read: John 6:25-40

Listen: What is God saying to you through his word today? Write about it in your journal.

Reflect: Crowds had come, hungering for the life and the fullness for which they were created. They were listening intently to the one who spoke so winsomely and provocatively about the kingdom of God. They were hanging on every word, trying desperately to get their fill of this *manna* which had come down from heaven.

And Jesus provided it. Not only did he give them words of life to satisfy their souls, but bread and fish to satisfy their bodies as well—and with plenty to spare.

He *took* the bread, *blessed* it, *broke* it, and *gave* it, just as he would do with the disciples in the upper room the night before his betrayal and death. But it didn't stop there. As he gave them the loaves and the fish, he just kept on giving. He gave and he gave and he gave. In fact, he gave so much that it fed thousands of people and there were still twelve full baskets of pieces left over. One for each of the twelve disciples. One representing each of the twelve tribes of Israel. God had a long history of providing bread for his people and here he was doing it again.

And just moments after he crossed the lake, here he was again talking about bread, reminding the religious leaders of the sacred place it held in the life of Israel. It was a powerful symbol of their constant hunger for God and God's constant willingness to provide. But "do not work for bread that spoils," he warned them, "but for food that endures to eternal life, which the Son of Man will give to you."

"Sir, give us this bread," they replied.

To which he responded, "I am the bread of life. He who comes to me will never go hungry, and he who believes in me will never be thirsty." But they did not believe him, so they starved themselves, continually trying to feed themselves on "bread" that could never satisfy their hungry souls. I guess not much has changed in two thousand years, huh?

Respond: What does it mean to you that Jesus is the bread of life? How do you feed on him? Will you?

Pray: Ask Jesus to show you what you feed on other than him. Ask him to give you the bread of life. Taste it, and see that the Lord is good.

Lord Jesus, help me to feed on you and not on all of the other things, and other people, I am tempted to feed on. Be my living bread today.

Rest: Rest in the presence of the One who sees you, knows you, and loves you.

February 28

Silence: Silence is the first movement toward the God who is always moving toward us. When we are silent it helps us to be more aware of and attentive to what he is up to. Without silence it lessens the likelihood that we will be able to connect with him in any meaningful and transformative way.

Opening Prayer: O Great Light of the World, shine in my darkness, so that I can see you clearly and love you truly. Amen.

Read: John 8:12

Listen: What is God saying to you through his word today? Write about it in your journal.

Reflect: *"I am the light of the world. Whoever follows me will not walk in darkness, but will have the light of life."*

Have you ever tried to walk in the dark? It's not an easy thing to do, for when we *walk in darkness* we are not able to see the way. We are left to stumble and tumble and struggle our way through life, with the surety that, at some point, we will get lost along the way. For walking in darkness means that we have no real idea of where we are going and no real knowledge of who we are. We cannot even tell where we have been. Thus, we have no way of seeing the dangers, pitfalls, traps, and snares along the way. Needless to say, we are in desperate need of a light.

Then along comes Jesus, the light of the world. It's just who he is. It's part of his divinely unique character. Wherever Jesus is present, he shines his light. As a result, whoever follows him no longer walks in darkness, but has the light of life. His light enables us to see people and things as they really are. His light reveals the truth about all things: our God, ourselves, and our world.

But in order to see clearly, we must continue to stay close to him, lest we wander away from the light of his love. For apart from him, all is darkness. And the further we get away from him, the darker the darkness becomes.

Respond: What does I AM the light of the world mean to you? How are you experiencing Jesus as the light of the world? Are you walking closely to that light these days?

Pray: Imagine Jesus as the light of the world. Sit before him in prayer and allow him to shine his light on you and in you. What do you to see?

O Jesus, light of the world, thank you that we never have to walk in darkness, but can have the light of life through you. Help us to walk in that light today and every day. Amen.

Rest: Rest in the presence of the One who sees you, knows you, and loves you.

February 29

Silence: We can really only become still and quiet before God if we trust that everything is under his control. Give God all of those things that are worrying and concerning you today. Trust him with all that is on your mind and in your heart. "Cast all of your cares upon him because he cares for you."

Opening Prayer: Lord Jesus, thank you that you offer us a safe and secure place to rest in you. Help us to enjoy that space today. Help us to enjoy you, even as you enjoy us.

Read: John 10:1-10

Listen: What is God saying to you through his word today? Write about it in your journal.

Reflect: *"I tell you the truth, I am the gate for the sheep." (John 10:7)*

Out in the fields, the shepherd would lie down in the opening of the sheep pen in order to keep the sheep safe and keep them from wandering off. Thus, the shepherd himself was the gate.

That is the image Jesus is using here. It's meant to tell us something special about his divine character. *"I AM the gate for the sheep,"* he tells us. Thus, he is the one who lays down his life in order to provide for, protect, and defend his precious lambs. He offers them a safe place where they can lie down in green pastures and sit beside still waters. He gives a space where the can rest secure. He is both the entrance and the exit to the pen. They come and go at his bidding and his call.

By contrast, the one who is a thief and a robber tries to climb in by some other way. He is bent on the sheep's destruction. His intent is to kill, steal, and destroy. But the sheep need not worry, for they are protected by the gate, who is also their shepherd. He came to guard and protect and provide. He came that the sheep may have life, and have it to the full.

Respond: What does it mean to you that Jesus is the gate? How does that help you to rest secure in him?

Pray: Rest in the security of your God. Enjoy the safe space he has created for you. Allow your fears and insecurities to subside and simply enjoy him.

Thank you, Lord Jesus, that you are the gate for the sheep. Help me to rest safe and secure in your love today. Amen.

Rest: Rest in the presence of the One who sees you, knows you, and loves you.

March 1

Silence: Take a few minutes and allow your soul to *lie down in green pastures* and to *sit beside still waters*. Let God breathe his life into you. Just sit and take it in. This is how the soul is restored.

Opening Prayer: The Lord is my shepherd, I shall not want. He makes me lie down in green pastures, he guides me beside still waters, he restores my soul. He guides me in paths of righteousness for his name's sake.

Even though I walk through the valley of the shadow of death, I will not fear, for you are with me; your rod and your staff, they comfort me.

You prepare a table before me in the presence of my enemies. You anoint my head with oil; my cup overflows. Surely goodness and love will pursue me all the days of my life, and I will dwell in the house of the Lord forever. (Psalm 23:1-6)

Read: John 10:11-18

Listen: What is God saying to you through his word today? Write about it in your journal.

Reflect: *"I AM the good shepherd. The good shepherd lays his life down for the sheep."*

"I AM the good shepherd; I know my sheep and my sheep know me."

There is a beautiful mutuality in this picture. It is a mutuality that flows out of the very heart of God — beginning in creation and continuing on to consummation.

We were made out of the overflow of divine love. God was so full of love that he could not contain himself, so he created us, in order to share in the very heart and life and intimacy of the Trinity. In other words, God created us to love and to be loved, to know and to be known — *just as the Father knows me and I know the Father.* That's some pretty deep knowing.

God created us for relationship, and his divine purposes can only be fulfilled in relationship. That's why the image of a shepherd and his sheep is such a beautiful and tender one. There are no lengths he will not go to in order to show his love for us, including laying down his life. That's what a good shepherd does.

Respond: What does it mean to you that God is your good shepherd? How does that play out in your relationship with him? What difference will it make in the way you see him and relate to him today?

Pray: Thank God for being your good shepherd. Thank him for the ways he *has* shepherded you in the past, the ways he *is* shepherding you in the present, and the ways he *will* shepherd you in the future. Thank him for laying down his life for his sheep.

Lord Jesus, our Good Shepherd, thank you that you love us so much that you would lay down your life in order that we might spend forever together in eternity. Since you have so gladly done this for us, please show us how we need to lay down our lives for others.

Rest: Rest in the presence of the One who sees you, knows you, and loves you.

March 2

Silence: Spend a few minutes in silence, letting your heart and your mind come to rest. Take a few deep breaths and relax your body. Once you come to a sense of stillness, proceed with the opening prayer.

Opening Prayer: Lord Jesus, thank you that you are the resurrection and the life, which means that death does not have the final word—life does. It is the paschal mystery: death always brings about new life. Thanks be to God!

Read: John 11:17-27

Listen: What is God saying to you through his word today? Write about it in your journal.

Reflect: *"I AM the resurrection and the life. Whoever believes in me will live, even though he dies; and whoever lives and believes in me will never die. Do you believe this?"*

There's an awful lot of pain in this world. At times it feels like death and destruction is all there is. It can feel overwhelmingly dark and desperate. It's easy for us to ask the question, "Where is God in the midst of it all?"

Then along comes Jesus. He enters into our sorrow and sadness, he stands with us in our brokenness and tears, and he weeps over our pain and grief. Our heartbreak breaks his heart as well, but it doesn't stop there. For in the midst of all the suffering and sadness and death, he proclaims: "I AM the resurrection and the life. I bring life out of death, I bring beauty out of ashes, I bring joy out of sorrow, and I bring hope out of despair. Wherever you see or experience death, rest assured that I am at work brining about new life, even out of the most tragic and awful of circumstances. Don't lose heart because I AM with you. I AM bringing about something good and beautiful and eternal. It's just who I AM. Do you believe this? Well, do you?"

Respond: What does it mean to you that Jesus is the resurrection and the life? Do you believe it? Where and how have you experienced it?

Pray: Mediate for a few minutes on Jesus' statement: "I AM the resurrection and the life." Ask God to help you believe it. Ask him to give you eyes to see how and where and when he has brought new life out of death, both in you and around you.

Thank you, Lord Jesus, that you are the resurrection and the life. Give me eyes to see the ways and the places you have brought new life out of death.

Rest: Rest in the presence of the One who sees you, knows you, and loves you.

March 3

Silence: First there is silence, then God speaks, and then things come into being. It has been that way since creation began and it will be that way again today. So, silence your heart and mind in preparation for God to speak.

Opening Prayer: Thank you, Lord Jesus, that we don't need to know the way, we just need to know you because you are the way and the truth and the life. If we just follow you, we'll find everything we are looking for.

Read: John 14:1-11

Listen: What is God saying to you through his word today? Write about it in your journal.

Reflect: *"I AM the way, the truth, and the life. No one comes to the Father except through me." (John 14:6)*

"Lord, we don't know where you are going, so how can we know the way?" What a great question! But instead of giving answers, Jesus just gives himself. "I AM the way and the truth and the life," he says. "Don't worry about knowing the way, just know me. For not only am I the way, but I am also the truth and the life. If you want to really know the way to the Father, you must follow me."

Lest we think that Jesus is just the gate, he tells us that he is also the way. We cannot just enter the gate and forget about him; we must also walk in his way. That's where truth and life is found.

As Thomas à Kempis so beautifully said, "Without the Way there is no going, without the Truth there is no knowing, without the Life, there is no living." I don't know about you, but I want all of the above. Thanks be to God that he gives us all of these things through Jesus.

Respond: What does it mean to you that Jesus is the way? What does it mean to you that Jesus is the truth? What does it mean to you that Jesus is the life? How are these three interconnected?

Pray: Spend a few minutes mediating on Jesus as the way. Spend a few minutes mediating on Jesus as the truth. Now spend a few minutes meditating on Jesus as the life. Pay attention to what is stirring in you as a result.

Thank you, Lord Jesus, that you are the way and the truth and the life. Thank you that the way we come to the Father, and the way we come to know the Father, is through you. Help us to know you better and better each day. Help us to know you, even as we are known.

Rest: Rest in the presence of the One who sees you, knows you, and loves you.

March 4

Silence: Spend a few minutes in silence allowing your soul and spirit to come to stillness before God. This will prepare your heart to receive whatever he may have for you today.

Opening Prayer: Lord Jesus, forgive me when I begin to think that I can do this life on my own; I cannot. Apart from you I can do nothing. Help me to abide in you this day, even as you abide in me. For only then can my life and my ministry bear the fruit it was meant to bear.

Read: John 15:1-8

Listen: What is God saying to you through his word today? Write about it in your journal.

Reflect: *"I AM the vine; you are the branches. If anyone abides in me and I in him, he will bear much fruit; apart from me you can do nothing." (John 15:5)*

More than anything I want deep connection with you, and you with me. This life that we share is meant to be about intimate, passionate union. I want you to be so interconnected with me that no one can tell where you end and where I begin, because your life is not really your life at all, but my life in and through you. That's how it works; that's how my life within you grows and flourishes — through abiding deeply in me. It is also how you bear fruit for the kingdom. After all, apart from me you can do nothing.

Respond: Who or what are you abiding in these days? What is the fruit of that abiding? What would it look like to abide in Jesus? How can you do that? Will you?

Pray: Pray today that God would continually make you aware of and attentive to the life of his Spirit within you. Ask him to help you to do every task and speak every word out of a deep inner connectedness with him, so that all you do, think, or say — no matter how mundane or ordinary or trivial it may seem — would be done for his kingdom and his glory.

Be the vine, Lord Jesus, and help me to be the branch. Help me to learn how to abide in you today, so that I might learn to abide in you every minute of every day. Amen.

Rest: Rest in the presence of the One who sees you, knows you, and loves you.

March 5

Silence: It all starts with silence—always with silence. Allow yourself to become still and quiet before God. This may take a few minutes, so don't rush it. Once you are ready, open yourself up to God, and to whatever he may have for you today.

Opening Prayer: "One thing I ask of the Lord, this is what I seek: that I may dwell in the house of the Lord all the days of my life, to gaze upon the beauty of the Lord and to seek him in his temple." (Ps. 27:4)

Read: Psalm 27:1-5

Listen: What is God saying to you through his word today? Write about it in your journal.

Reflect: In the midst of chaos—evil men advancing, enemies attacking, armies besieging, and war breaking out—David asks for *one thing*, and it's probably not the one thing you would expect. Instead of asking God to intervene, or make it all go away, he asks that he might "dwell in the house of the Lord all the days of his life, to gaze upon the beauty of the Lord and to seek him in his temple."

He does not ask for his circumstances to change; he asks for his perspective to change. He asks for his practice to change. David knows the value of *beholding;* it's a spiritual practice. He knows that if he can learn to dwell in God's house and gaze upon God's beauty and seek God in his temple, then everything else will take care of itself.

The problem is that it's really easy to talk about doing those things, and even to write about them, and maybe even to pray about them, without actually doing them. Take it from me, I've become an expert. There are many days when I pray this very prayer and think about its beauty and write about its wisdom and its depths, without actually taking the time to stop and dwell and gaze and seek. And if I fail to actually do those things, they cannot bear fruit in my life.

G. K. Chesterton once said, "The difference between talking about prayer and praying, is the same as the difference between blowing a kiss and kissing." If we don't actually do it, we will never reap the benefits, or taste the pleasures, of true intimacy with God. Which is so sad for us, but even sadder for God. God longs for us to know the depths and breadth and heights and passion and intimacy and delights of his unfailing love.

It's almost like God is waiting for us to bask in his love and express our love for him in return, but all we do is talk about it or think about it or write about it. We never really enter into it. Thus, he's left saying, "Are you going to kiss me or what? Are you going to dwell and gaze and seek, or are you just going to sit there? Are you just going to think about it, or are you actually going to do it? Don't just talk about loving me—love me!

Respond: What do the words dwell, gaze, and seek mean to you? How do they take shape in your time with him? How often do you actually do them? How often do you make time and space to dwell with God, to gaze upon his beauty, and to seek him in his temple?

Pray: Ask the Lord to help you to learn how to dwell in his house, gaze upon his beauty, and seek him in his temple. Ask him for the time and space and discipline to do them.

Forgive me, O Lord, when I talk about dwelling and gazing and seeking, and fail to do them. Help me to make time and space today to do the *one thing* David asked.

Rest: Rest in the presence of the One who sees you, knows you, and loves you.

March 6

Silence: We live in a noisy and chaotic world. It's a world in which we are likely to be consumed by all the things within us and around us that are constantly clamoring for our attention. Come to silence this morning and give God your undivided attention and affection.

Opening Prayer: O God, help us to truly know you, so that we might become all you desire us to be. Amen.

Read: 1 Corinthians 13:12

Listen: What is God saying to you through his word today? Write about it in your journal.

Reflect: God always invites us beyond where we are. Thus, as we embrace the invitation deeper into his heart, it is both very exciting and absolutely terrifying. That's because as we go deeper into him, he asks us to let go of deeper and deeper things. Some of which are so deep that they feel like part of who we are, but they are not. They are merely the most subtle and deceptive ways we have lived falsely.

Moving deeper into the heart of God means that we learn to be our truest, most Christ-like selves, not merely some false or manufactured version of that. Which means that sometimes this call to wholeness means letting go of what our idea of wholeness even looks like in the first place.

It is all a part of the journey to "know fully, even as we are fully known." The two go hand in hand. God does not want us to settle for anything less, so whatever it takes to strip away the false and bring about the true is what God's going to do. He loves us too much to allow us to live lives that are less than what he dreamt them to be.

Respond: What does it mean for you to know God, even as you are fully known? What is the next level of *knowing* that he is inviting you to? How does knowing him fully enable you to know yourself fully?

Pray: Take some time to mediate on what it means to know God, even as you are fully known. Ask him to bring about that kind of knowing in your heart, soul, and mind

Lord God, seeing you and knowing you is such a process; it does not happen all at once. So please lead me on this incredible journey of knowing and being known, until that day when I am able to see you clearly and know you — and myself — fully. Amen.

Rest: Rest in the presence of the One who sees you, knows you, and loves you.

March 7

Silence: Silence wakes us up to God's voice and God's Spirit. It helps us to be able to see him and hear him more clearly. If we refuse to enter into silence, we do so at our own expense. Be silent before the Lord this morning and give him the time and the space to speak and work and act in you.

Opening Prayer: O my God, Trinity whom I adore, help me forget myself entirely so to establish myself in you, unmovable and peaceful as if my soul were already in eternity. May nothing be able to trouble my peace or make me leave you, O my unchanging God, but may each minute bring me more deeply into your mystery! Grant my soul peace. Make it your heaven, your beloved dwelling and the place of your rest. May I never abandon you there, but may I be there, whole and entire, completely vigilant in my faith, entirely adoring, and wholly given over to your creative action. ~Elizabeth of the Trinity

Read: Matthew 3:13-17

Listen: What is God saying to you through his word today? Write about it in your journal.

Reflect: *"This is my Son, whom I love; with him I am well pleased."* *(Mt.3:17)*

Jesus was the beloved Son of God, and God did not want him, or anyone else, to ever forget that. So just before Jesus was sent into the desert of his temptation, God spoke, reminding him of that beautiful truth. It would be the only food he would have to feed on over the next forty days. It was also the truth that would give him strength to fight the voices that would assault him in the wilderness, saying, "If you really are the Son of God, then…"

God knew just what Jesus needed: "You are my son, whom I love. With you I am well pleased." And those words were not only true for him, but true for us as well. Particularly as we battle the voices in our heads, our hearts, and our world that would have us believe otherwise.

I don't know about you, but I invest a lot of time and energy trying to convince myself and my world that I am worthy of being loved. If I could somehow convince myself that I am God's beloved, it would certainly make life a lot easier and a lot less complicated.

Do you believe that you are God's beloved? Do you really? Will you claim your belovedness today?

Respond: Jesus was the beloved of God, do you really believe that you are as well? Will you claim your belovedness today? Will you help others to discover their belovedness?

Pray: Listen to the voice of Him who calls you his beloved.

Father, thank you that I am your child, whom you love, and in whom you are well pleased.

Rest: Rest in the presence of the One who sees you, knows you, and loves you.

March 8

Silence: Sit for a few minutes in silence, allowing the light of God to rise in your heart. This will illuminate whatever it is that he wants you to see, and help you to hear whatever it is that he may want you to hear.

Opening Prayer: Thank you, Lord Jesus, that you always call us beyond where we are. Help us to never get too comfortable or too familiar or too secure that we settle for less of a life with you than you want. Challenge us and draw us deeper and deeper into you.

Read: Luke 5:1-11

Listen: What is God saying to you through his word today? Write about it in your journal.

Reflect: You are constantly calling us beyond where we are, constantly drawing us and challenging us to total trust and absolute surrender.

You call us out of the shallows and into the deep. You call us to the place where we are in way over our heads; to the place where we are no longer in control, but have to completely commit all of ourselves, our lives, and our well-being to you alone.

You call us beyond our own efforts and our own toiling, in order to show us what can happen when we live our lives according to your will, your way, and your direction. You bring us to the end of ourselves, so that we can find the beginnings of you.

You are ever expanding our picture and our experience of you. You are ever stretching us and challenging us by taking us to places where we have no choice but to see you as you really are, so that we might begin to see ourselves as we really are. Your desire is that we, like Simon Peter, might make the shift from merely calling you "Master," to calling you "Lord."

You call us to leave behind our boats and our nets and our fish — even our very lives — in order that we might follow you. You call us away from a life of merely catching fish, to a life of catching men and women.

Help us to hear and to heed. Give us the courage and the grace and the strength to hear your call upon our lives, pull our boats up on the shore, and unreservedly leave everything behind in order to follow you. You will settle for nothing less, and neither should we.

Respond: How is Jesus calling you deeper into life with him? What does that look like? What will you need to leave behind?

Pray: Hear the call of Jesus upon your life today. Ask him what it looks like for you to take him up on this invitation to follow him in a new and deeper way. Will you?

Lord Jesus, never let me settle for less of a life than the life you want for me. Never allow me to be content with following you partially, rather than following you fully. You are not a half-way kind of God, so help me not to operate under the illusion that I can be a half-way kind of follower. Give me the courage to fully follow you, whatever that may mean.

Rest: Rest in the presence of the One who sees you, knows you, and loves you.

March 9

Silence: Sit and wait for a few minutes for *the God who comes*. Clear your thoughts and still your soul, so that you are open and ready for his coming. Come, Lord Jesus!

Opening Prayer: Lord Jesus, give us the grace and the wisdom and strength to always keep our lamps burning, to always be awake and alert and attentive, to always be watching the door, waiting for your knock, so that when you arrive, we can open the door and let you in.

Read: Luke 12:35-40

Listen: What is God saying to you through his word today? Write about it in your journal.

Reflect: There is a flame within each of us, started and sustained by God's Spirit, which we are required to tend. It is the part of us that burns for God, for intimacy with him, and for his Kingdom to be revealed in this world. In some this fire is a raging inferno. In fact, it is so real and so present that if you get within a certain proximity of these people you will be warmed by the heat of its passion. And in others this fire is weak and smoldering, like a dim wick that is on the verge of being snuffed out completely. It is of no use to anyone. It provides no light and provides no warmth.

And though we cannot control the source of this fire, we are called to tend, feed, and fan its flame. We are called to make sure we *keep our lamps burning*. Therefore, we must be thoughtful and intentional as we consider how to nurture and grow this fire of God within us.

We must learn to listen and to reflect and to pray in ways that allow us to create the proper conditions for this fire to thrive, and for its flames to grow. We must regularly ask ourselves certain questions like: "What are the things that keep my inner fires going? When and how will I make those things a regular part of my life? What fuels my soul to keep me stumbling toward love? Who are the people and what are the practices that ignite something deep within me?"

And when we finally begin to get a sense of the answers to some of these questions, we need to go to work. We need to start gathering these logs and tossing them on the fire.

Respond: What is the state of your inner flame these days? How are you attempting to tend and stoke the life of God within you?

Pray: Ask God to ignite the flame of desire deep in your soul. Ask him what he wants you to do, in order to tend and stoke that inner flame. Ask him to help you know when and how he may be knocking on the door of your life, and what it looks like to open the door and let him in.

Lord Jesus, help my soul burn with a consuming desire for you and you alone.

Rest: Rest in the presence of the One who sees you, knows you, and loves you.

Conclusion

Thank you for joining me in this season of the journey. It has been a joy and a privilege to walk alongside you. I am grateful for your time, attention, and companionship.

As we close out this leg of our journey, I would love for you to take some time and reflect back on what God has stirred up in you over the past 40+ days. What stands out the most? How have you beheld Jesus? What did that help you see about yourself? What effect did that have on your heart, soul, and life?

Is a particular word, image, or theme emerging? What were the moments of consolation (joy, inspiration, gladness, or discovery) and what caused them? What were the moments of desolation (disruption, distress, disorientation, frustration, or sadness) and what brought those about?

I guess the bottom line is: What do you think God up to, and what is he inviting you into as a result?

Write a little about it in the pages provided, or write about it in your journal.

May His peace be with you.

Notes

Notes

Notes

Made in United States
Orlando, FL
20 January 2025